Naae

MAY -- 2018

Secret-Layer Cakes

Hidden Fillings & Flavors That Elevate Your Desserts

Dini Kodippili

Founder of The Flavor Bender

PAGE STREET
PUBLISHING CO.

PAGE STREET
PUBLISHING CO.

Copyright © 2017 Dini Kodippili

First published in 2017 by

Page Street Publishing Co.

27 Congress Street, Suite 105

Salem, MA 01970

www.pagestreetpublishing.com

Distributed by Macmillan, sales in Canada by The Canadian Manda Group.

21 20 19 18 17   1 2 3 4 5

ISBN-13: 978-1-62414-477-6

ISBN-10: 1-62414-477-2

Library of Congress Control Number: 2017937024

Cover and book design by Page Street Publishing Co.

Photography by Dini Kodippili

Printed and bound in China

To my husband, Kasun,
for being my biggest cheerleader.
You deserve all the cake.

Contents

No-Bake Cakes — 139

Ice Cream Cakes — 157

Introduction

Baking isn't just another form of cooking for me. As old and cliché as this may sound, ever since I learned to bake when I was really young, baking has enriched my life at every turn, filling it with untold hours of joy and satisfaction. My mother was my first teacher, introducing me to a nifty world where I could transform everyday ingredients like flour, sugar and eggs into a culinary work of art that delighted my friends and family and, of course, myself. Sure, a few of those early "masterpieces" resembled little more than the site of a crash landing, but they always tasted amazing!

And through all the ups and downs in life, baking has been my crutch, my therapy and my creative outlet. Whether it was to celebrate a birthday or a wedding or a graduation, or to pull myself through a rough patch, baking a cake seemed like the most perfect thing in the world to do. And why wouldn't it be? Throughout the rich history of cake baking, cakes have been synonymous with one thing—celebration. A celebration of new beginnings, of good times, of accomplishments, of love. If food were a language, cakes would no doubt mean "You matter to us. We love you."

One of my favorite things to bake when I was growing up was my cookie-bottomed chocolate cake, a sinfully fudgy chocolate cake and a cookie, all in one. My family loved it; my friends went nuts for it. So pretty soon, I was experimenting with my baking, incorporating various elements into my cakes, such as different ingredients, flavors, textures, types of cuisines and even altogether different types of desserts! I think my love of all things science made it even more fun (I've always been bit of a nerd, often geeking out at things that other people would find either amusing or confusing), so combining cakes with different layers that came together beautifully to make one scrumptious cake was incredibly exciting. Of course, they looked like regular cakes from the outside, covered in frosting, so seeing people's surprise when they cut into it to discover a whole new layer of indulgence hiding behind the curtains of frosting was very rewarding.

This also became the motivation and impetus behind my blog, theflavorbender.com, where I share recipes that combine different food elements in new and creative ways, with a focus on desserts, breakfast, brunch and, of course, flavor. This book, in turn, is an attempt to explore how you can use cake as a vehicle to combine all of that good stuff in creative and surprising ways. Here you will find cakes, cheesecakes, brownies, blondies, meringues, custards, mousses, jellies, cookies, pies and ice cream cakes, along with other elements of surprise like fruits, nuts, candy, booze and spices. Each recipe makes a fantastic cake worthy of celebration!

I absolutely adore the idea of two types of dessert in one slice, but seamlessly incorporating a brownie layer into a regular cake can be a little tricky for someone who hasn't tried it before, but it is by no means difficult. The collection of secret layer cake recipes that you will find in this book is meant to be accessible to anyone who'd like to surprise loved ones with a delicious homemade cake—whether it's the ten thousandth one they've baked or the very first one. I have strived to make my directions as clear and instructive as possible, so that you can follow along easily and make these fun desserts with secret layers that will wow your guests.

I hope you love reading and baking from this book just as much as I did writing it. There's no party without cake, so let's get started!

Why Secret—Layer Cakes and How to Use This Book

It's no secret that food relies on all of our senses to deliver its magic. Sight and taste are obvious ones, but smell, sound and texture are just as important for elevating the flavor profile of anything we eat. Layered cakes are an excellent vehicle to engage all of these senses because they incorporate a variety of different elements. I'm a huge advocate of great flavor, not just taste, and these cake recipes have been designed to capitalize on the power of flavor. The idea behind making secret layers is simple. It adds to the overall experience of eating these beautiful desserts. Pleasant and tasty surprises are always welcome in my household, and a lot of my readers enjoy them too, judging by all the feedback I have gotten on my blog. Cakes are celebratory in purpose, and with these recipes I have strived to make them even more joyful, flavorful and whimsical in execution.

How to Use This Book

First and foremost, remember the five Ps—proper preparation prevents poor performance. And that preparation includes reading the recipe from start to finish and making sure, before you start, that you have all the ingredients and amounts that the recipe calls for. This will prevent any frustrating surprises, disappointment and stress. It will also give you a sense of timing, an idea of what to expect and when to expect it.

The next most important thing when it comes to baking is timing. Yes, as all bakers will tell you, baking is a science to an extent, but it isn't rocket science. The times I have indicated in these recipes are very close approximations, but of course there are several variables when it comes to baking. Oven and ambient temperatures in your kitchen are key among them. I have sprinkled these recipes throughout with visual cues on doneness, so that you can look for those cues in addition to the time. Maybe your cake needs a few minutes more (or less) in the oven than what the recipe calls for. This is also why it's handy to cultivate some baking instincts as you go. Listen to your gut from time to time—after all, that's where these baked goodies go in the end anyway.

I have also included a chapter on commonly used techniques, with tips and tricks for different layers, which will help you produce great results every time. Make sure you read this chapter, so you understand the techniques involved in getting perfect results. It also goes without saying that quality ingredients and accurate measurements are vital for great baked goodies, so I have included a couple of brief chapters on commonly used ingredients and measurement conversions, while highlighting the importance of using a basic kitchen scale for your dry ingredients. I switch between the types of measurements used in order to give you the most accurate way of measuring out your ingredients, which in turn will give you the best chance for perfect results every time.

Finally, these secret-layer cake recipes are meant to provide you with a great canvas on which to build flavors and textures. From fillings, ganaches, frostings and crusts to all the different layers like brownies, blondies, meringues, custards, mousses, ice creams, cakes and cheesecakes, the different combinations of flavors and textures that you can develop with these recipes are endless! So don't be afraid to experiment and be adventurous. Once you have tried a couple of these recipes and you're familiar with the process, go ahead and mix it up, try a new combination or develop a flavor profile that you like. Make these recipes your own. What you will find within the pages of this book are cake ideas as much as recipes. So go where your flights of flavor fancy take you. You'll be pleasantly surprised.

Cheesecakes

I cannot imagine anyone not loving cheesecake. Smooth, creamy, decadent and delicious—it's comfort dessert for me. And I still remember the first time I ever ate cheesecake! I loved it so much that I introduced it to my little sister, and it soon became a thing for us. We would pool enough money to buy a cheesecake, sneak it into the house and then into our room, and eat the whole thing in one go, just between the two of us—with two forks and no plates.

But do you know what's even better than cheesecake? Combining my two favorite desserts—cheesecake and brownie—in one glorious layered dessert. Imagine cutting into a cheesecake only to find another indulgent, fudgy layer of brownie, hiding under the covers. Or a secret, delicious layer of meringue, candied bacon or chocolate chip cookie.

I hope these secret layer cheesecakes bring you just as much joy as they continue to bring me, and that you enjoy them with someone you love, with two forks and no plates.

Buckeye Brownie Cheesecake

Of all the chocolate combos out there, chocolate and peanut butter is a sacred one. This cheesecake is the proud product of a buckeye candy and a peanut butter cup marriage! Fudgy brownie and creamy peanut butter cheesecake—a simple combo that's any peanut butter and chocolate lover's dream!

Makes one 8–inch (20–cm) cake

Brownie Bottom

115 g (4 oz) bittersweet chocolate

115 g (4 oz) unsalted butter

¼ tsp salt

142 g (5 oz) granulated sugar

1 tsp vanilla extract

2 eggs

94 g (3.3 oz) all-purpose flour

142 g (5 oz) mini peanut butter cups, cut in half

Peanut Butter Cheesecake

455 g (16 oz) cream cheese, softened

100 g (3.5 oz) granulated sugar

180 g (6.3 oz) peanut butter

2 tsp (6 g) cornflour (cornstarch)

¾ cup (177 ml) whipping cream

Pinch of salt

1 tsp vanilla extract

3 eggs

Brownie Bottom

Preheat the oven to 350°F (180°C). Butter an 8-inch (20-cm) wide, 3-inch (8-cm) tall springform pan, line the bottom with parchment paper and dust the sides with flour.

Melt the chocolate, butter and salt together in a heatproof bowl in 30-second intervals in the microwave, until nice and smooth. Stir in the granulated sugar and vanilla, and let cool slightly.

Add the eggs, one at a time, and whisk until fully incorporated. Fold in the flour and halved peanut butter cups until just combined. Pour into the prepared pan. Bake for 15 minutes.

Remove from the oven, and let cool for at least 10 to 15 minutes. Reduce the oven temperature to 300°F (150°C) to bake the cheesecake.

Peanut Butter Cheesecake

While the brownie layer is baking, get the cheesecake layer ready.

In a bowl using a hand mixer, whip the cream cheese and granulated sugar until creamy and smooth. Add the peanut butter, cornflour, cream, salt and vanilla and mix on medium speed until well combined and the batter is nice and smooth with no lumps. Add the eggs, one at a time, and whisk on slow speed or manually with a balloon whisk (taking care not to overbeat).

Pour the cheesecake batter over the slightly cooled brownie layer. Tightly double wrap the bottom of your springform pan with two pieces of foil. Then place the springform pan in a larger baking tray (that can easily fit the 8-inch [20-cm] pan), and fill the baking tray with hot water (really hot tap water will do). The water level should be about halfway up the sides of the springform pan, and make sure that the water doesn't seep through the foil. Place the baking tray in the oven and bake for 60 to 70 minutes, until the cheesecake is set but slightly jiggly in the middle when you shake it gently.

Turn off the oven, and let the cheesecake cool for 15 to 30 minutes while still inside the oven with the oven door left ajar (this way the residual heat helps cook the cheesecake a tad further, plus you don't have to handle the cake while it's too hot).

Remove the cheesecake from the oven and the water bath, and let cool to room temperature completely; this can take up to 4 hours, depending on the ambient room temperature.

(continued)

Buckeye Brownie Cheesecake (cont.)

Chocolate Ganache

340 g (12 oz) semisweet chocolate, chopped or chips

1 cup (236 ml) whipping cream

Pinch of salt

Peanut Butter Glaze

57 g (2 oz) unsalted butter

Pinch of salt

180 g (6.3 oz) peanut butter

85 g (3 oz) confectioners' sugar

To Decorate

Mini peanut butter cups, cut in half (optional)

Gently loosen the cheesecake from the pan. If the cheesecake is sticking slightly to the pan, you can run a thin butter knife along the edge of the pan to loosen the cake. Cover the cheesecake and refrigerate for at least 8 hours or overnight.

Chocolate Ganache

Place the semisweet chocolate in a heatproof bowl. Add the cream and salt to the chocolate and microwave in 30-second intervals, stirring in between, until the chocolate has melted.

Mix to make sure the ganache is smooth and let cool to a thick, spreadable consistency. You can keep the chocolate ganache in the fridge to speed the cooling process.

Peanut Butter Glaze

Melt the butter, salt and peanut butter in a heatproof bowl in the microwave in 30-second intervals, stirring in between. Add the confectioners' sugar and mix until smooth. The glaze will thicken as it cools. Let cool to a spreadable consistency.

Decorate

Once chilled, transfer the cheesecake to a serving dish. Spread the chocolate ganache along the sides and spread the peanut butter glaze on top, and then decorate with extra peanut butter cups, if desired.

Hummingbird Lemon Cheesecake

The sweet, tropical flavor of pineapple paired with banana bread is always a winner for me, which is why I love a good hummingbird cake. This blondie version is definitely fudgier than the cake version, and adds a delicious tropical twist to a classic lemon cheesecake.

Makes one 8–inch (20–cm) cake

Hummingbird Cake Blondie

170 g (6 oz) overripe bananas

115 g (4 oz) unsalted butter

115 g (4 oz) brown sugar

¼ tsp salt

½ tsp ground cinnamon

2 eggs

115 g (4 oz) crushed pineapple, drained

1 tsp vanilla extract

57 g (2 oz) walnuts, chopped

57 g (2 oz) all-purpose flour

Lemon Cheesecake

455 g (16 oz) cream cheese, softened

2 tsp (6 g) cornflour (cornstarch)

115 g (4 oz) granulated sugar

Pinch of salt

¼ cup (59 ml) whipping cream

¼ cup (60 ml) lemon juice

1 tsp finely grated lemon zest

1 tsp vanilla extract

3 eggs

Hummingbird Cake Blondie

Preheat the oven to 350°F (180°C). Butter an 8-inch (20-cm) wide, 3-inch (8-cm) tall springform pan. Line the bottom with parchment paper and dust the sides with flour.

Mash up the bananas in a bowl. Melt the butter, brown sugar and salt together in a separate heatproof bowl in 30-second intervals in the microwave. Once melted, stir to form a smooth butter-sugar mixture. Set aside to let cool a bit.

When the sugar mixture has cooled, add the mashed bananas and cinnamon and stir to combine. Add the eggs one at a time, and whisk well after each addition. Fold in the crushed pineapple, vanilla and walnuts. Fold in the flour until just combined.

Pour the batter into the prepared pan and bake for 20 minutes. Remove the blondie from the oven, and let cool for at least 10 to 15 minutes. Lower the oven temperature to 300°F (150°C) to bake the cheesecake.

Lemon Cheesecake

While the blondie layer is baking, get the cheesecake layer ready.

In a mixing bowl using a hand mixer, whip the cream cheese, cornflour and granulated sugar together until smooth and creamy. Add the salt, cream, lemon juice, zest and vanilla to the cheesecake batter and mix on medium speed until all the ingredients have combined well and the mixture is smooth.

Add the eggs one at a time, and mix on low speed, or manually with a balloon whisk, until fully incorporated (take care not to overbeat).

Pour the cheesecake batter over the slightly cooled blondie layer. Tightly double wrap the bottom of your springform pan with two pieces of foil. Then place the springform pan in a larger baking tray (that can easily fit the 8-inch [20-cm] pan) and fill the baking tray with hot water (really hot tap water will do). The water level should be about halfway up the sides of the springform pan, and make sure that the water doesn't seep through the foil. Carefully place the baking tray in the oven and bake for 60 to 70 minutes, until the cheesecake is set but slightly jiggly in the middle when you shake it gently.

Turn off the oven, and let the cheesecake cool for 15 to 30 minutes while inside the oven with the oven door ajar (this way the residual heat helps cook the cheesecake a tad further, plus you don't have to handle the cake while it's too hot).

(continued)

Hummingbird Lemon Cheesecake (cont.)

Stabilized Whipped Cream

3 tbsp (44 ml) water

1½ tsp (5 g) powdered gelatin

2 cups (473 ml) plus 1 tbsp (15 ml) chilled whipping cream, divided

½ cup (65 g) confectioners' sugar

1 tsp vanilla

To Decorate

Pineapple pieces

Chopped walnuts

Remove the cheesecake from the oven and the water bath and let cool to room temperature; this can take up to 4 hours, depending on the ambient room temperature.

Gently loosen the cheesecake from the pan. If the cheesecake is sticking slightly to the pan, you can run a thin butter knife along the edge of the pan to loosen the cake. Cover the cheesecake and refrigerate for at least 8 hours or overnight.

Stabilized Whipped Cream

When ready to assemble the cake, place the water in a small heatproof bowl and evenly sprinkle the gelatin over it. Set aside for 10 to 15 minutes to let the gelatin bloom. Microwave the bloomed gelatin in 10-second intervals, stirring in between, until the gelatin is completely dissolved (it's important that you don't let the gelatin boil).

Add 2 cups (473 ml) of the chilled whipping cream and confectioners' sugar to a cold bowl. Whisk with the whisk attachment of your hand mixer on medium speed. Add the remaining 1 tablespoon (15 ml) of chilled cream to the hot, dissolved gelatin mix. Add this gradually to the cream that is being whipped (being careful to pour it *near* the whisk, so that the gelatin gets mixed in with the cream immediately!). Add the vanilla and whisk on medium speed until you get stiff peaks, and use it immediately.

Decorate

Once the cheesecake is chilled, spread the stabilized whipped cream on the sides of the cake and pipe a whipped cream border on the top of the cake. Top with pineapple pieces and chopped walnuts.

Cookie Monster's Cheesecake

I imagine Cookie Monster's favorite cheesecake would be cookies and cream. So I bet he'd love this even more with that chocolate chip cookie base! This is a fun cheesecake to make for kids. That bright blue color with crushed oreos will have little cookie monsters jumping for joy everywhere.

Makes one 8–inch (20–cm) cake

Chocolate Chip Cookie Blondie

115 g (4 oz) unsalted butter

½ tsp salt

75 g (2.6 oz) brown sugar

1 egg

1 tsp vanilla extract

125 g (4.4 oz) all-purpose flour, divided

115 g (4 oz) semisweet mini chocolate chips

Cookies and Cream Cheesecake

455 g (16 oz) cream cheese, softened

2 tsp (6 g) cornflour (cornstarch)

100 g (3.5 oz) granulated sugar

Pinch of salt

½ cup (118 ml) whipping cream

Blue gel food coloring

1 tsp vanilla extract

3 eggs

15 regular Oreo cookies, crushed into small pieces

Chocolate Chip Cookie Blondie

Preheat the oven to 350°F (180°C). Butter an 8-inch (20-cm) wide, 3-inch (8-cm) tall springform pan, line the bottom with parchment paper and dust the sides with flour.

Melt the butter, salt and brown sugar in a heatproof bowl in the microwave in 30-second intervals, stirring in between. Mix to form a smooth butter-sugar mix. Set aside to cool slightly.

When the sugar mix has cooled, add the egg and vanilla, and whisk until fully mixed. Add half of the flour and fold it into the blondie batter. Add the other half along with the chocolate chips and fold to combine (the blondie batter will be quite thick).

Place the batter in the prepared pan and spread it evenly. Bake for 15 minutes. Remove from the oven, and let cool for at least 10 to 15 minutes. Reduce the oven temperature to 300°F (150°C) to bake the cheesecake.

Cookies and Cream Cheesecake

While the blondie layer is baking, get the cheesecake layer ready.

In a bowl using a hand mixer, whip the cream cheese, cornflour and granulated sugar until smooth and creamy. Add the salt, cream, a few drops of blue coloring and vanilla and mix on medium speed until the ingredients have combined well and the mix is smooth. Add more blue coloring as needed to get that deep blue Cookie Monster color. Add the eggs, one at a time, and mix on low speed or manually with a balloon whisk until fully incorporated. Add the crushed Oreos and fold to combine (take care not to overbeat).

Pour the cheesecake batter over the slightly cooled blondie layer. Tightly double wrap the bottom of your springform pan with two pieces of foil. Then place the springform pan in a larger baking tray (that can easily fit the 8-inch [20-cm] pan), and fill the baking tray with hot water (really hot tap water will do). The water level should be about halfway up the sides of the springform pan, and make sure that the water doesn't seep through the foil. Place the baking tray in the oven and bake for 60 to 70 minutes, until the cheesecake is set but slightly jiggly in the middle when you shake it gently.

Turn off the oven, and let the cheesecake cool for 15 to 30 minutes while still inside the oven with the oven door left ajar (this way the residual heat helps cook the cheesecake a tad further, plus you don't have to handle the cake while it's too hot).

(continued)

Cookie Monster's
Cheesecake (cont.)

Chocolate Ganache

170 g (6 oz) semisweet chocolate chips

½ cup (118 ml) whipping cream

Pinch of salt

To Decorate

Chocolate chip cookies, broken up into pieces

Remove the cheesecake from the oven and the water bath, and let cool to room temperature completely; this can take up to 4 hours, depending on the ambient room temperature.

Gently loosen the cheesecake from the pan. If the cheesecake is sticking slightly to the pan, you can run a thin butter knife along the edge of the pan to loosen the cake. Cover the cheesecake and refrigerate for at least 8 hours or overnight.

Chocolate Ganache

Place the semisweet chocolate in a heatproof bowl. Add the cream and salt and microwave in 30-second intervals, stirring in between, until the chocolate has melted. Mix to make sure the ganache is smooth and then let cool to a thick but spreadable consistency. You can keep the chocolate ganache in the fridge to speed the cooling process.

Decorate

Once the cheesecake is chilled, spread the chocolate ganache on the sides of the cheesecake, and then cover the surface on top as well. It's OK if it's not completely smooth on top because it'll be covered with chocolate chip cookies anyway. When the ganache has set, decorate with chocolate chip cookie pieces on top, and serve.

Praline Crust Spiced Poached Pear Cheesecake

This cheesecake is a party in your mouth. The crust is extra crunchy, sweet, salty and over-the-top delicious. Those perfectly poached pears taste even better when smothered with creamy, spiced cheesecake. This cake is so good, it's absolutely worth using your good wine to make it!

Makes one 8—inch (20—cm) cake

Spiced Poached Pears

2 cups (473 ml) good-quality Merlot red wine (or a good medium- or full-bodied red wine)

½ cup (118 ml) orange juice

100 g (3.5 oz) granulated sugar

4 cloves

1 cinnamon stick

4 ripe but firm Bosc pears, peeled, quartered and cored

Praline Crust

115 g (4 oz) unsalted butter

½ tsp kosher salt

115 g (4 oz) brown sugar

142 g (5 oz) graham cracker squares (14–16 crackers)

⅓ cup (40 g) chopped pecans (or walnuts)

42 g (1.5 oz) unsalted butter, melted

Spiced Poached Pears

Combine the red wine, orange juice, granulated sugar, cloves and cinnamon stick in a saucepan over medium-high heat. Bring the wine to a boil, stirring. Place the quartered pears in the poaching liquid, lower the heat and simmer for 30 minutes, turning them over once halfway through, to make sure the pears are completely poached.

Turn off the heat and let the pears cool in the poaching liquid.

Remove the pears from the poaching liquid (the poached pears can be used right away, or you can store the drained pears in the fridge in an airtight container, to be used the following day).

Return the poaching liquid to a boil. Simmer for 15 to 30 minutes, until the liquid thickens into a syrup. Discard the cloves and cinnamon stick. Refrigerate until needed.

Praline Crust

Preheat the oven to 350°F (180°C). Butter an 8-inch (20-cm) wide, 3-inch (8-cm) tall springform pan, line the bottom with parchment paper and dust the sides with flour.

Melt the butter, salt and brown sugar in a saucepan over medium heat. Whisk to form a smooth butter-sugar mix. Let the mix come to a boil, and then continue to boil over medium heat for 2 to 3 minutes.

While the butter-sugar mix is cooking, line a quarter sheet pan (9 x 13 inches [23 x 33 cm]) with parchment paper, and place the graham cracker squares in one layer to fit the pan. Pour the hot butter-sugar mix evenly over the crackers, using a spatula to spread the mix evenly. Sprinkle the chopped nuts over the graham crackers. Transfer to the oven and bake for 10 to 12 minutes (you should see the toffee bubbling along the edges of the pan, but do not let it burn). Remove from the oven and let cool completely, until the toffee hardens.

Break the toffee into squares and transfer them to a food processor. Pulse to crush the toffee squares. Add the melted butter to the graham cracker crumbs and process to mix.

Press the crushed toffee squares into the bottom of the pan to form a crust. Freeze for about 30 minutes (or in the fridge overnight) to let the crust harden.

(continued)

Praline Crust Spiced Poached Pear Cheesecake (cont.)

Spiced Cheesecake

455 g (16 oz) cream cheese, softened

2 tsp (6 g) cornflour (cornstarch)

100 g (3.5 oz) granulated sugar

Pinch of salt

½ cup (118 ml) whipping cream

¼ tsp ground cloves

½ tsp ground cinnamon

Zest of 1 orange

1 tsp vanilla extract

3 eggs

White Chocolate Ganache

200 g (7 oz) white chocolate chips

¼ cup (59 ml) whipping cream

Pinch of salt

Spiced Cheesecake

In a bowl using a hand mixer, whip the cream cheese, cornflour and granulated sugar until creamy and smooth. Add the salt, cream, ground cloves, ground cinnamon, orange zest and vanilla and mix on medium speed until the ingredients are combined and the mix is smooth. Add the eggs, one at a time, and mix on low speed or manually with a balloon whisk until fully incorporated (but take care not to overbeat).

Remove the quartered and poached pears from the fridge and blot 8 pear pieces with a paper towel to remove excess moisture.

Take the praline crust from the freezer (or fridge) and place the 8 pear quarters on the crust, with the pointed ends in the center and the bottoms radiating out, and all 8 pieces facing up or down. Do not let the pears touch the edge of your springform pan. Pour the cheesecake batter over the poached pears. Gently shake the pan to make the top even.

Tightly double wrap the bottom of your springform pan with two pieces of foil. Then place the springform pan in a larger baking tray (that can easily fit the 8-inch [20-cm] pan), and fill the baking tray with hot water (really hot tap water will do). The water level should be about halfway up the sides of the springform pan, and make sure that the water doesn't seep through the foil. Place the baking tray in the oven and bake for 60 to 70 minutes, until the cheesecake is set but slightly jiggly in the middle when you shake it gently.

Turn off the oven, and let the cheesecake cool for 15 to 30 minutes while still inside the oven with the oven door left ajar (this way the residual heat helps cook the cheesecake a tad further, plus you don't have to handle the cake while it's too hot).

Remove the cheesecake from the oven and the water bath, and let cool to room temperature completely; this can take up to 4 hours, depending on the ambient room temperature.

Gently loosen the cheesecake from the pan. If the cheesecake is sticking slightly to the pan, you can run a thin butter knife along the edge of the pan to loosen the cake. Cover the cheesecake and refrigerate for at least 8 hours or overnight.

White Chocolate Ganache

In a heatproof bowl, heat the white chocolate, cream and salt in the microwave in 30-second intervals, stirring in between, until the chocolate chips have melted. Stir until you have a smooth ganache. Let cool slightly until it reaches a spreadable consistency.

Decorate

Once chilled, transfer the cheesecake to a serving dish. Spread the white chocolate ganache along the sides and place the remaining 8 cold poached pear quarters on top of the chilled cheesecake (in any direction or pattern you fancy.) Drizzle the red wine syrup on top.

Biscoff Blondie Coffee Cheesecake

If a lazy afternoon could have flavor, this is probably what it would taste like: a cup of coffee with Biscoff cookies. I love the flavor that the Biscoff cookies add to the blondie bottom, and it goes really well with the creamy, coffee-flavored cheesecake. A great dessert for the coffeeholics in your life.

Makes one 8—inch (20—cm) cake

Biscoff Blondie

226 g (8 oz) unsalted butter

½ tsp salt

175 g (6.2 oz) brown sugar

115 g (4 oz) Biscoff cookies, finely ground in the food processor

2 eggs

1 tsp vanilla extract

190 g (6.7 oz) all-purpose flour

Coffee Cheesecake

455 g (16 oz) cream cheese, softened

2 tsp (6 g) cornflour (cornstarch)

142 g (5 oz) granulated sugar

2 tsp (2 g) instant coffee granules

½ cup (118 ml) whipping cream

Pinch of salt

1 tsp vanilla extract

2 eggs

1 egg yolk

Biscoff Blondie

Preheat the oven to 350°F (180°C). Butter an 8-inch (20-cm) wide, 3-inch (8-cm) tall springform pan. Line the bottom with parchment paper and dust the sides with flour.

Melt the butter, salt and brown sugar in a heatproof bowl in 30-second intervals in the microwave. Stir to form a smooth butter-sugar mix. Set aside to cool slightly.

Once the sugar mix has cooled, stir in the ground Biscoff cookies. Add the eggs, one at a time, and whisk well after each addition. Stir in the vanilla. Add the flour to the blondie batter and fold it in to combine.

Pour the batter into the prepared pan and bake for 20 minutes.

Remove blondie from the oven, and let cool for at least 10 to 15 minutes. Reduce the oven temperature to 300°F (150°C) to bake the cheesecake.

Coffee Cheesecake

While the blondie layer is baking, get the cheesecake layer ready.

In a bowl using a hand mixer, whip the cream cheese, cornflour and granulated sugar until smooth and creamy. Dissolve the instant coffee in the cream. Add the salt, coffee cream and vanilla to the cheesecake batter and mix on medium speed until the ingredients have combined well and the mix is smooth. Add the eggs and egg yolk, one at a time, and mix on low speed or manually with a balloon whisk until fully incorporated. Do not overbeat.

Pour the cheesecake batter over the slightly cooled blondie layer. Tightly double wrap the bottom of your springform pan with two pieces of foil. Then place the springform pan in a larger baking tray (that can easily fit the 8-inch [20-cm] pan), and fill the baking tray with hot water (really hot tap water will do). The water level should be about halfway up the sides of the springform pan, and make sure that the water doesn't seep through the foil. Place the baking tray in the oven and bake for 60 to 70 minutes, until the cheesecake is set but slightly jiggly in the middle when you shake it gently.

Turn off the oven, and let the cheesecake cool for 15 to 30 minutes while still inside the oven with the oven door left ajar (this way the residual heat helps cook the cheesecake a tad further, plus you don't have to handle the cake while it's too hot).

(continued)

Biscoff Blondie Coffee Cheesecake (cont.)

Stabilized Whipped Cream

2 tbsp (30 ml) water

¾ tsp powdered gelatin

1 cup (236 ml) plus ½ tbsp (7 ml) chilled whipping cream, divided

2 tbsp (16 g) confectioners' sugar

To Decorate

Biscoff cookies

Melted chocolate

Cocoa powder

Remove the cheesecake from the oven and the water bath, and let cool to room temperature completely; this can take up to 4 hours, depending on the ambient room temperature.

Gently loosen the cheesecake from the pan. If the cheesecake is sticking slightly to the pan, you can run a thin butter knife along the edge of the pan to loosen the cake. Cover the cheesecake and refrigerate for at least 8 hours or overnight.

Stabilized Whipped Cream

When ready to assemble, place the water in a small bowl and evenly sprinkle the gelatin over it. Set aside for 10 to 15 minutes to let the gelatin bloom.

Microwave the bloomed gelatin in 10-second intervals, stirring in between, until the gelatin is completely dissolved (take care not to let the gelatin boil).

Add 1 cup (236 ml) of the chilled whipping cream and the confectioners' sugar to a cold bowl. Whisk with the whisk attachment of your hand mixer on medium speed. Add the remaining ½ tablespoon (7 ml) of chilled cream to the hot, dissolved gelatin mix. Add this gradually to the cream that is being whipped (being careful to pour it near the whisk, so that the gelatin gets mixed in with the cream immediately!). Whisk gently until you get stiff peaks. Use immediately.

Decorate

Once the cheesecake is chilled, spread a layer of whipped cream on top. Spread the melted chocolate on the backs of the Biscoff cookies and stick them on the sides of the chilled cheesecake just before serving (this will prevent the cookies from getting soggy). Dust the top with some cocoa powder.

Coconut Cardamom Cheesecake

This cheesecake is inspired by two classic Sri Lankan desserts—watalappan (coconut cardamom custard) and bibikkan (coconut fruit cake). It's a molassey and fruity cake bottom topped with a creamy spiced coconut cheesecake. It's different from the classic, but uniquely delicious.

Makes one 8—inch (20—cm) cake

Coconut Cake

170 g (6 oz) muscovado sugar

¼ tsp ground cardamom

¼ tsp ground ginger

100 g (3.5 oz) desiccated coconut

¼ cup (59 ml) coconut milk

1 tsp vanilla extract

Pinch of salt

2 eggs

70 g (2.5 oz) chopped dates

70 g (2.5 oz) raisins

100 g (3.5 oz) fine semolina

30 g (1 oz) all-purpose flour

Spiced Coconut Cheesecake

455 g (16 oz) cream cheese, softened

2 tsp (6 g) cornflour (cornstarch)

115 g (4 oz) muscovado sugar

Pinch of salt

½ cup (122 ml) coconut cream

½ tsp ground cardamom

Coconut Cake

Preheat the oven to 350°F (180°C). Butter and line the bottom of an 8-inch (20-cm) springform pan with parchment paper and dust the sides with flour.

Place the muscovado sugar, cardamom, ginger, coconut and coconut milk in a saucepan. Heat over medium heat until the sugar is completely dissolved. Transfer the sugar-coconut mix to a bowl. Add the vanilla, salt, eggs, dates and raisins and mix to combine. Fold in the semolina and flour to combine.

Spread the batter evenly on the bottom of the prepared pan. Bake in the oven for 15 minutes. Remove from the oven, and let cool for at least 10 to 15 minutes. Reduce the oven temperature to 300°F (150°C) to bake the cheesecake.

Spiced Coconut Cheesecake

While the cake layer is baking, get the cheesecake layer ready.

In a bowl using a hand mixer, whip the cream cheese, cornflour and muscovado sugar together until creamy and smooth. Add the salt, coconut cream, cardamom, cinnamon and coconut and mix on medium speed until the ingredients are well combined and the batter is smooth. Add the eggs, one at a time, and mix on low speed or manually with a balloon whisk until fully incorporated (take care not to overbeat).

Pour the cheesecake batter over the slightly cooled coconut cake layer. Tightly double wrap the bottom of your springform pan with two pieces of foil. Then place the springform pan in a larger baking tray (that can easily fit the 8-inch [20-cm] pan), and fill the baking tray with hot water (really hot tap water will do). The water level should be about halfway up the sides of the springform pan, and make sure that the water doesn't seep through the foil. Place the baking tray in the oven and bake for 60 to 70 minutes, until the cheesecake is set but slightly jiggly in the middle when you shake it gently.

Turn off the oven, and let the cheesecake cool for 15 to 30 minutes while still inside the oven with the oven door left ajar (this way the residual heat helps cook the cheesecake a tad further, plus you don't have to handle the cake while it's too hot).

(continued)

Coconut Cardamom Cheesecake (cont.)

¼ tsp ground Ceylon cinnamon (use regular cinnamon if you cannot find Ceylon cinnamon)

56 g (2 oz) desiccated coconut

3 eggs

To Decorate

Whipped coconut cream

Roasted cashews

Remove the cheesecake from the oven and the water bath, and let cool to room temperature completely; this can take up to 4 hours, depending on the ambient room temperature.

Gently loosen the cheesecake from the pan. If the cheesecake is sticking slightly to the pan, you can run a thin butter knife along the edge of the pan to loosen the cake. Cover the cheesecake and refrigerate for at least 8 hours or overnight.

Assembly

Before serving, top the cheesecake with whipped coconut cream and roasted cashews.

Blackout Brownie
Red Velvet Cheesecake

This cheesecake is a homage to my favorite holiday of the year—Halloween! The black cocoa gives the brownie a natural black color and it's perfect for Halloween. The red ganache also adds to that "bloody" appearance. Feel free to make this cake even more whimsical with candy eyes and other Halloween decorations when you share it with friends and family.

Makes one 8—inch (20—cm) cake

Fudgy Blackout Brownie

115 g (4 oz) unsalted butter

71 g (2.5 oz) granulated sugar

71 g (2.5 oz) brown sugar

2 eggs

1 tsp vanilla extract

43 g (1.5 oz) black cocoa powder, sifted

Pinch of salt

60 g (2.1 oz) all-purpose flour

Red Velvet Cheesecake

455 g (16 oz) cream cheese, softened

2 tsp (6 g) cornflour (cornstarch)

100 g (3.5 oz) granulated sugar

Pinch of salt

1 tbsp (15 ml) white vinegar

½ cup (118 ml) whipping cream

1 tbsp (7 g) natural cocoa powder

Red gel food coloring

1 tsp vanilla extract

2 eggs

1 egg yolk

Fudgy Blackout Brownie

Preheat the oven to 350°F (180°C). Butter an 8-inch (20-cm) wide, 3-inch (8-cm) tall springform pan. Line the bottom with parchment paper and dust the sides with flour.

Melt the butter in the microwave in 30-second intervals, stirring in between. Add the granulated and brown sugars and mix thoroughly until the batter has cooled and thickened.

Add the eggs, one at a time, whisking each one well before adding the next. Add the vanilla, sifted cocoa powder, salt and all-purpose flour and mix gently.

Pour the batter into the prepared cake pan and bake for 20 minutes. Remove the brownie layer from the oven and let cool for 10 to 15 minutes. Lower the oven temperature to 300°F (150°C) to bake the cheesecake.

Red Velvet Cheesecake

While the brownie layer is baking, get the cheesecake layer ready.

In a bowl using a hand mixer, whip the cream cheese, cornflour and granulated sugar until creamy and smooth. Add the salt, white vinegar, cream, cocoa powder, a few drops of red coloring and vanilla and mix on medium speed until the ingredients are well combined and the batter is smooth. Add the eggs and egg yolk, one at a time, and mix on low speed or manually with a balloon whisk until fully incorporated. Add a few more drops of red coloring if needed, and whisk to combine (be careful not to overbeat).

Pour the cheesecake batter over the slightly cooled brownie layer. Tightly double wrap the bottom of your springform pan with two pieces of foil. Then place the springform pan in a larger baking tray (that can easily fit the 8-inch [20-cm] pan), and fill the baking tray with hot water (really hot tap water will do). The water level should be about halfway up the sides of the springform pan, and make sure that the water doesn't seep through the foil. Place the baking tray in the oven and bake for 60 to 70 minutes, until the cheesecake is set but slightly jiggly in the middle when you shake it gently.

Turn off the oven, and let the cheesecake cool for 15 to 30 minutes while still inside the oven with the oven door left ajar (this way the residual heat helps cook the cheesecake a tad further, plus you don't have to handle the cake while it's too hot).

(continued)

Blackout Brownie
Red Velvet Cheesecake (cont.)

Red-Colored White Chocolate Ganache

200 g (7 oz) white chocolate chips

¼ cup (59 ml) whipping cream

Pinch of salt

Red gel food coloring

Stabilized Whipped Cream

3 tbsp (44 ml) water

1½ tsp (5 g) powdered gelatin

2 cups (473 ml) plus 1 tbsp (15 ml) chilled whipping cream, divided

¼ cup (33 g) confectioners' sugar

To Decorate

Black cocoa powder, to sift on top

Remove the cheesecake from the oven and the water bath, and let cool to room temperature completely; this can take up to 4 hours, depending on the ambient room temperature.

Gently loosen the cheesecake from the pan. If the cheesecake is sticking slightly to the pan, you can run a thin butter knife along the edge of the pan to loosen the cake. Cover the cheesecake and refrigerate for at least 8 hours or overnight.

Red-Colored White Chocolate Ganache

Place the white chocolate chips in a heatproof bowl. Add the cream and salt, and microwave in 30-second intervals, stirring in between, until the chocolate has melted. Add a few drops of red coloring and mix through to get a deep red color. Mix to make sure the ganache is smooth and then let cool slightly to a thick but pourable consistency.

Stabilized Whipped Cream

When ready to assemble, place the water in a small bowl and evenly sprinkle the gelatin over it. Set aside for 10 to 15 minutes to let the gelatin bloom.

Microwave the bloomed gelatin in 10-second intervals, stirring in between, until the gelatin is completely dissolved (take care not to let the gelatin boil).

Add 2 cups (473 ml) of the chilled whipping cream and the confectioners' sugar to a cold bowl. Whisk with the whisk attachment of your hand mixer on medium speed. Add the remaining 1 tablespoon (15 ml) of chilled cream to the hot, dissolved gelatin mix. Add this gradually to the cream that is being whipped (being careful to pour it near the whisk, so that the gelatin gets mixed in with the cream immediately!). Whisk gently until you get stiff peaks.

Place the whipped cream in a pastry bag with an open or closed star pastry tip. Use immediately.

Decorate

When the cheesecake is chilled, spread the red-colored white chocolate ganache on the sides of the cheesecake and on the top. Let the ganache set. Pipe whipped cream swirls along the top border of the cheesecake. Refrigerate until you're ready to serve, and sift extra black cocoa on top of the cheesecake just before serving.

Butterscotch Bananas Foster Cheesecake

Bananas Foster is such a simple yet satisfying dessert to make whenever cravings hit. I especially love this cheesecake version because it's a banana cake, banana pudding and bananas Foster all in one. The overripe bananas add an almost rum-like flavor to the cheesecake.

Makes one 8–inch (20–cm) cake

Butterscotch Blondie

170 g (6 oz) unsalted butter

½ tsp kosher salt

200 g (7 oz) brown sugar

2 eggs

1 tsp vanilla extract

85 g (3 oz) finely chopped walnuts

115 g (4 oz) butterscotch chips

180 g (6.3 oz) all-purpose flour

Bananas Foster Cheesecake

226 g (8 oz) overripe bananas (2–3 bananas)

455 g (16 oz) cream cheese, softened

¼ cup (59 ml) whipping cream

2 tsp (6 g) cornflour (cornstarch)

70 g (2.5 oz) granulated sugar

⅓ cup (79 ml) rum

Pinch of salt

¼ tsp ground cinnamon

2 tsp (10 ml) vanilla extract

2 eggs

1 egg yolk

Butterscotch Blondie

Preheat the oven to 350°F (180°C). Butter an 8-inch (20-cm) wide, 3-inch (8-cm) tall springform pan, line the bottom with parchment paper and dust the sides with flour.

Melt the butter, salt and brown sugar in a heatproof bowl in the microwave in 30-second intervals. Stir to form a smooth butter-sugar mix. Set aside to let cool slightly.

When the sugar mix has cooled, add the eggs, one at a time, and whisk well after each addition to fully mix in each egg. Stir in the vanilla and then fold in the walnuts, butterscotch chips and flour.

Pour the batter into the prepared pan and bake for 20 minutes. Remove from the oven, and let cool for at least 10 to 15 minutes. Reduce the oven temperature to 300°F (150°C) to bake the cheesecake.

Bananas Foster Cheesecake

While the blondie layer is baking, get the cheesecake layer ready.

Using a fork or hand mixer, mash the bananas until fairly smooth. A few lumps are OK. Add the cream cheese, cream, cornflour and granulated sugar and mix until creamy and smooth. Next, add the rum, salt, cinnamon and vanilla and mix on medium speed until the ingredients are well combined and the batter is smooth. Add the eggs and egg yolk, one at a time, and mix on low speed or manually with a balloon whisk until fully incorporated (be sure not to overbeat).

Pour the cheesecake batter over the slightly cooled blondie layer. Tightly double wrap the bottom of your springform pan with two pieces of foil. Then place the springform pan in a larger baking tray (that can easily fit the 8-inch [20-cm] pan), and fill the baking tray with hot water (really hot tap water will do). The water level should be about halfway up the sides of the springform pan, and make sure that the water doesn't seep through the foil. Place the baking tray in the oven and bake for 60 to 70 minutes, until the cheesecake is set but slightly jiggly in the middle when you shake it gently.

Turn off the oven, and let the cheesecake cool for 15 to 30 minutes while still inside the oven with the oven door left ajar (this way the residual heat helps cook the cheesecake a tad further, plus you don't have to handle the cake while it's too hot).

(continued)

Butterscotch Bananas Foster Cheesecake (cont.)

Butterscotch Sauce

115 g (4 oz) unsalted butter

½ tsp kosher salt

115 g (4 oz) brown sugar

½ cup (118 ml) whipping cream

2 tsp (10 ml) vanilla extract

Stabilized Whipped Cream

3 tbsp (44 ml) water

1½ tsp (5 g) powdered gelatin

2 cups (473 ml) plus 1 tbsp (15 ml) chilled whipping cream, divided

¼ cup (33 g) confectioners' sugar

To Decorate

Banana slices

Remove the cheesecake from the oven and the water bath, and let cool to room temperature completely; this can take up to 4 hours, depending on the ambient room temperature.

Gently loosen the cheesecake from the pan. If the cheesecake is sticking slightly to the pan, you can run a thin butter knife along the edge of the pan to loosen the cake. Cover the cheesecake and refrigerate for at least 8 hours or overnight.

Butterscotch Sauce

Melt the butter, salt and brown sugar in a saucepan over medium heat. Whisk to make sure you have a smooth sauce and the sugar is completely dissolved. Add the cream while whisking, and then reduce the heat to medium-low. Whisk to combine and bring the mixture to a boil. Let the butterscotch sauce boil gently for 10 to 15 minutes, stirring frequently, until the sauce thickens. Stir in the vanilla. Let the butterscotch sauce cool completely before using. If the butterscotch sauce thickens too much, heat it gently with a splash of cream until you get the desired consistency.

Stabilized Whipped Cream

When ready to assemble the cake, place the water in a small heatproof bowl and evenly sprinkle the gelatin over it. Set aside for 10 to 15 minutes to let the gelatin bloom.

Microwave the bloomed gelatin in 10-second intervals, stirring in between, until the gelatin is completely dissolved (it's important that you don't let the gelatin boil).

Add 2 cups (473 ml) of the chilled whipping cream and confectioners' sugar to a cold bowl. Whisk with the whisk attachment of your hand mixer on medium speed. Add the remaining 1 tablespoon (15 ml) of chilled cream to the hot, dissolved gelatin mix. Add this gradually to the cream that is being whipped (being careful to pour it near the whisk, so that the gelatin gets mixed in with the cream immediately!). Whisk on medium speed until you get stiff peaks, and use it immediately.

Place half of the whipped cream in a pastry bag with an open or closed star pastry tip. Use immediately.

Decorate

Once the cheesecake is chilled, spread the stabilized whipped cream on the sides of the cheesecake. Pipe the top border of the cheesecake with the whipped cream in the pastry bag. Decorate with banana slices, and then drizzle butterscotch sauce on top.

milk and Cookies
Cheesecake

To turn this classic combination into a secret-layer cake, I turned to mascarpone cheese, which has a very creamy, milky taste compared to cream cheese. The bottom layer in this cake is one giant chocolate chip cookie with crisp edges and a fudgy center. So forget cookies and milk—if you want to be Santa's favorite, leave him a slice of this cheesecake next time.

Makes one 8—inch (20—cm) cake

Chocolate Chip Cookie Blondie

115 g (4 oz) unsalted butter

½ tsp salt

75 g (2.6 oz) brown sugar

1 egg

1 tsp vanilla extract

125 g (4.4 oz) all-purpose flour, divided

115 g (4 oz) semisweet mini chocolate chips

Milk Cheesecake

226 g (8 oz) cream cheese

226 g (8 oz) mascarpone cheese

75 g (2.6 oz) granulated sugar

Pinch of salt

½ cup (118 ml) whipping cream

1 tsp vanilla extract

2 eggs

1 egg yolk

To Decorate

Mini chocolate chip cookies (5–6.4 cm [2"–2½"] in diameter)

Melted chocolate

Chocolate Chip Cookie Blondie

Preheat the oven to 350°F (180°C). Butter an 8-inch (20-cm) wide, 3-inch (8-cm) tall springform pan, line the bottom with parchment paper and dust the sides with flour.

Melt the butter, salt and brown sugar in a heatproof bowl in 30-second intervals in the microwave. Stir to form a smooth butter-sugar mix. Set aside to cool slightly. When the sugar mix has cooled, add the egg and vanilla, and whisk until fully mixed. Add half of the flour and fold it into the batter. Add the other half along with the chocolate chips and fold in to combine (the batter will be quite thick).

Scrape the batter into the prepared pan and spread it evenly. Bake for 15 minutes. Remove from the oven and let cool for at least 10 to 15 minutes. Reduce the oven temperature to 300°F (150°C) to bake the cheesecake.

Milk Cheesecake

While the blondie layer is baking, get the cheesecake layer ready. In a bowl using a hand mixer, whip the cream cheese, mascarpone and granulated sugar until creamy and smooth. Add the salt, cream, and vanilla and mix on medium speed until the ingredients have combined and the batter is smooth. Add the eggs and egg yolk, one at a time, and mix on low speed or manually with a balloon whisk until fully incorporated (take care not to overbeat).

Pour the cheesecake batter over the slightly cooled blondie layer. Tightly double wrap the bottom of your springform pan with two pieces of foil. Then place the springform pan in a larger baking tray (that can easily fit the 8-inch [20-cm] pan), and fill the baking tray with hot water about halfway up. Place the baking tray in the oven and bake for 60 to 70 minutes.

Turn off the oven, and let the cheesecake cool for 15 to 30 minutes while still inside the oven with the oven door left ajar (this way the residual heat helps cook the cheesecake a tad further, plus you don't have to handle the cake while it's too hot). Remove the cheesecake from the oven and the water bath, and let cool to room temperature completely; this can take up to 4 hours, depending on the ambient room temperature.

Gently loosen the cheesecake from the pan. If the cheesecake is sticking slightly to the pan, you can run a thin butter knife along the edge of the pan to loosen the cake. Cover the cheesecake and refrigerate for at least 8 hours or overnight.

Decorate

When the cheesecake is chilled, spread a little melted chocolate on the backs of the mini chocolate chip cookies and stick on the sides of the cake.

Pistachio Rose Saffron Cheesecake

Saffron is such an incredible spice! Yes, it's expensive, which is why I was exposed to it quite sparingly growing up. But I was recently reintroduced to this beautiful spice thanks to my friend Shadi, and now I can't get enough of it. This cheesecake is inspired by the flavors and spices of Persian cooking. It's a fudgy pistachio blondie paired with a delicately spiced, floral cheesecake. Plus, this is naturally gluten-free.

Makes one 8–inch (20–cm) cake

Pistachio Blondie

170 g (6 oz) unsalted butter

Pinch of salt

94 g (3.3 oz) brown sugar

94 g (3.3 oz) granulated sugar

2 eggs

170 g (6 oz) raw pistachios

100 g (3.5 oz) almond flour

1 tsp vanilla extract

Saffron Rose Cheesecake

10–12 strands of saffron

100 g (3.5 oz) plus ¼ tsp granulated sugar, divided

2 tbsp (30 ml) boiling water

455 g (16 oz) cream cheese, softened

½ cup (118 ml) whipping cream

2 tsp (6 g) cornflour (cornstarch)

3 tbsp (44 ml) rose water

⅛ tsp ground turmeric or a few drops of yellow food coloring (optional)

1 egg

2 egg yolks

Pistachio Blondie

Preheat the oven to 350°F (180°C). Butter an 8-inch (20-cm) wide, 3-inch (8-cm) tall springform pan, line the bottom with parchment paper and dust the sides with flour.

Melt the butter, salt, brown sugar and granulated sugar in a heatproof bowl in 30-second intervals in the microwave. Stir to form a smooth butter-sugar mix. Set aside to cool slightly.

When the sugar mix has cooled, add the eggs, one at a time, whisk after each egg until fully combined.

Place the pistachios in a food processor and pulse until mostly finely chopped. Fold the chopped pistachios, almond flour and vanilla into the blondie batter.

Pour the batter into the prepared pan and bake for 20 minutes. Remove the pan from the oven and let cool for at least 10 to 15 minutes. Reduce the oven temperature to 300°F (150°C) to bake the cheesecake.

Saffron Rose Cheesecake

While the blondie layer is baking, get the cheesecake layer ready.

Using a mortar and pestle, grind the saffron strands with the ¼ teaspoon sugar until the saffron threads are completely crushed. Add the hot water to the ground saffron threads and let it steep for at least 15 to 20 minutes.

In a large bowl, combine the cream cheese, saffron water, cream, remaining 100 grams (3.5 oz) of sugar, cornflour and rose water. Using a hand mixer, beat the ingredients on medium-high speed until creamy and smooth, 2 to 3 minutes. Add the turmeric or yellow food coloring if you'd like a deeper yellow color. Mix the cheesecake batter for another minute or two. Add the egg and egg yolks, one at a time, and mix on low speed or with a balloon whisk. When the eggs have completely mixed in, pour the cheesecake batter over the cooled pistachio blondie.

Tightly double wrap the bottom of your springform pan with two pieces of foil. Then, place the springform pan in a larger baking tray (that can easily fit the 8-inch [20-cm] pan), and fill the baking tray with hot water (really hot tap water will do). The water level should be about halfway up the sides of the springform pan, and make sure that the water doesn't seep through the foil. Place the baking tray in the oven and bake for 60 to 70 minutes, until the cheesecake is set but slightly jiggly in the middle when you shake it gently.

(continued)

Pistachio Rose Saffron Cheesecake (cont.)

Stabilized Whipped Cream

2 tbsp (30 ml) water

¾ tsp powdered gelatin

1 cup (236 ml) plus ½ tbsp (7 ml) chilled whipping cream, divided

2 tbsp (16 g) confectioners' sugar

To Decorate

Edible rose petals

Chopped pistachios

Turn off the oven, and let the cheesecake cool for 15 to 30 minutes while still inside the oven with the oven door left ajar (this way the residual heat helps cook the cheesecake a tad further, plus you don't have to handle the cake while it's too hot).

Remove the cheesecake from the oven and the water bath, and let cool to room temperature completely; this can take up to 4 hours, depending on the ambient room temperature.

Gently loosen the cheesecake from the pan. If the cheesecake is sticking slightly to the pan, you can run a thin butter knife along the edge of the pan to loosen the cake. Cover the cheesecake and refrigerate for at least 8 hours or overnight.

Stabilized Whipped Cream

When ready to assemble, place the water in a small bowl and evenly sprinkle the gelatin over it. Set aside for 10 to 15 minutes to let the gelatin bloom.

Microwave the bloomed gelatin in 10-second intervals, stirring in between, until the gelatin is completely dissolved (take care not to let the gelatin boil).

Add 1 cup (236 ml) of the chilled whipping cream and the confectioners' sugar to a cold bowl. Whisk with the whisk attachment of your hand mixer on medium speed. Add the remaining ½ tablespoon (7 ml) of chilled cream to the hot, dissolved gelatin mix. Add this gradually to the cream that is being whipped (being careful to pour it *near* the whisk, so that the gelatin gets mixed in with the cream immediately!). Whisk gently until you get stiff peaks. Transfer the whipped cream into a pastry bag with a large open star tip. Use immediately.

Decorate

Pipe the stabilized whipped cream on top of the cake and sprinkle the edible rose petals and pistachios on top. Serve.

Brownie Bottom
Irish Cream Cheesecake

All the flavors of Irish cream in indulgent cheesecake form with a fudgy brownie layer. I used Irish whiskey instead of Irish cream for this recipe. Why? Because Irish whiskey packs more of a punch, and who doesn't want that from a boozy cake? Sláinte!

Makes one 8–inch (20–cm) cake

Brownie Bottom

115 g (4 oz) bittersweet chocolate

115 g (4 oz) unsalted butter

140 g (5 oz) granulated sugar

¼ tsp salt

1 tsp vanilla extract

2 eggs

94 g (3.3 oz) all-purpose flour

Irish Cream Cheesecake

455 g (16 oz) cream cheese, softened

2 tsp (6 g) cornflour (cornstarch)

100 g (3.5 oz) granulated sugar

Pinch of salt (to enhance flavor, optional)

1 tbsp good-quality cocoa powder, sifted

¼ cup (59 ml) whipping cream

½ cup (118 ml) Irish whiskey

1 tsp vanilla extract

1 egg

2 egg yolks

Brownie Bottom

Preheat the oven to 350°F (180°C). Butter an 8-inch (20-cm) wide, 3-inch (8-cm) tall springform pan. Line the bottom with parchment paper and dust the sides with flour.

Melt the chocolate and butter in a heatproof bowl in 30-second intervals in the microwave, stirring in between to prevent the chocolate from burning. Let the chocolate-butter mix cool.

When the mixture has cooled, add the granulated sugar, salt and vanilla to the cooled chocolate-butter mix and whisk to combine. Add the eggs, one at a time, whisking each one really well before adding the next. Fold in the flour until just combined.

Pour the batter into the prepared cake pan and bake for 15 minutes. Remove from the oven and let cool for 10 to 15 minutes. Lower the oven temperature to 300°F (150°C) to bake the cheesecake.

Irish Cream Cheesecake

While the brownie layer is baking, get the cheesecake layer ready.

In a bowl using a hand mixer, whip the cream cheese, cornflour and granulated sugar until creamy and smooth. Add the salt, cocoa powder, cream, Irish whiskey and vanilla to the cheesecake batter and mix on medium speed until the ingredients are combined and the batter is smooth. Add the egg and egg yolks, one at a time, and mix on the lowest speed or manually with a balloon whisk until fully incorporated (do not overbeat).

Pour the cheesecake batter over the slightly cooled brownie layer. Tightly double wrap the bottom of your springform pan with two pieces of foil. Then place the springform pan in a larger baking tray (that can easily fit the 8-inch [20-cm] pan), and fill the baking tray with hot water (really hot tap water will do). The water level should be about halfway up the sides of the springform pan, and make sure that the water doesn't seep through the foil. Place the baking tray in the oven and bake for 60 to 70 minutes, until the cheesecake is set but slightly jiggly in the middle when you shake it gently.

Turn off the oven, and let the cheesecake cool for 15 to 30 minutes while still inside the oven with the oven door left ajar (this way the residual heat helps cook the cheesecake a tad further, plus you don't have to handle the cake while it's too hot).

Remove the cheesecake from the oven and the water bath, and let cool to room temperature completely; this can take up to 4 hours, depending on the ambient room temperature.

Gently loosen the cheesecake from the pan. If the cheesecake is sticking slightly to the pan, you can run a thin butter knife along the edge of the pan to loosen the cake. Cover the cheesecake and refrigerate for at least 8 hours or overnight.

(continued)

Brownie Bottom *Irish Cream* Cheesecake (cont.)

Chocolate Ganache (optional)

170 g (6 oz) semisweet chocolate, chopped or chips

⅓ cup (79 ml) whipping cream

2 tbsp (30 ml) Irish whiskey

Pinch of salt

Stabilized Whipped Cream

3 tbsp (44 ml) water

1½ tsp (5 g) powdered gelatin

2 cups (473 ml) plus 1 tbsp (15 ml) chilled whipping cream, divided

½ cup (65 g) confectioners' sugar

Chocolate Ganache

Place the semisweet chocolate in a heatproof bowl. Add the cream, whiskey and salt and microwave in 30-second intervals, stirring in between, until the chocolate has melted.

Mix to make sure the ganache is smooth and let cool to a thick, spreadable consistency.

Stabilized Whipped Cream

When ready to assemble the cake, place the water in a small heatproof bowl and evenly sprinkle the gelatin over it. Set aside for 10 to 15 minutes to let the gelatin bloom. Microwave the bloomed gelatin in 10-second intervals, stirring in between, until the gelatin is completely dissolved (it's important that you don't let the gelatin boil).

Add 2 cups (473 ml) of the chilled whipping cream and confectioners' sugar to a cold bowl. Whisk with the whisk attachment of your hand mixer on medium speed. Add the remaining 1 tablespoon (15 ml) of chilled cream to the hot, dissolved gelatin mix. Add this gradually to the cream that is being whipped (being careful to pour it near the whisk, so that the gelatin gets mixed in with the cream immediately!). Whisk on medium speed until you get stiff peaks. Transfer the whipped cream into a pastry bag with an open star tip. Use immediately.

Decorate

When the cheesecake has chilled, spread some of the thickened chocolate ganache evenly over the top. Let the ganache layer cool and set. Pipe a whipped cream border around the edge of the cheesecake. Refrigerate until ready to serve.

Cherry Pie Brownie Cheesecake

Delicious cherry pie swirled with fudgy brownie and cheesecake, this cake is nothing short of a cherry pie + brownie + cheesecake ménage à trois. Complete with caramelized pie crust pastry, this cake is a treat!

Makes one 8-inch (20-cm) cake

Cherry Pie Brownie Layer

170 g (5.9 oz) bittersweet chocolate

170 g (6 oz) unsalted butter

142 g (5 oz) sugar

¼ tsp salt

1 tsp vanilla extract

2 eggs

100 g (3.5 oz) all-purpose flour

85 g (3 oz) store-bought cherry filling

Cherry Pie Cheesecake

455 g (16 oz) cream cheese, softened

½ cup (118 ml) whipping cream

75 g (2.6 oz) sugar

1 tsp vanilla extract

2 tsp (6 g) cornflour (cornstarch)

1 egg

2 egg yolks

120 g (4.3 oz) store-bought cherry filling

Cherry Pie Brownie Layer

Preheat the oven to 350°F (180°C). Butter an 8-inch (20-cm) wide, 3-inch (8-cm) tall springform pan. Line the bottom with parchment paper and dust the sides with flour.

Melt the chocolate and butter in the microwave in 30-second intervals, stirring in between to prevent the chocolate from burning. Let the chocolate-butter mix cool.

When the mixture has cooled, add the sugar, salt and vanilla and whisk to combine. Next, add the eggs, one at a time, whisking well after each addition. Fold in the flour until just combined.

Pour the batter into the prepared cake pan and then spread the cherry pie filling on top. Bake for 15 minutes.

Remove the brownie layer from the oven and let cool for 10 to 15 minutes. Lower the oven temperature to 300°F (170°C) to bake the cheesecake.

Cherry Cheesecake Layer

While the brownie layer is baking, get the cheesecake layer ready.

Combine cream cheese, cream, sugar, vanilla and cornflour in a bowl. Using a hand mixer or stand mixer, whisk on medium speed until creamy and smooth with no lumps. On the lowest speed on the hand mixer, or with a whisk, add the egg and egg yolks and whisk until just combined (be careful not to overmix).

Pour the cheesecake batter on top of the cooled brownie, and dollop the cherry pie filling all over the cheesecake batter. Swirl and shake gently to smooth the top. Tightly double wrap the bottom of your springform pan with two pieces of foil. Then place the springform pan in a larger baking tray (that can easily fit the 8-inch [20-cm] pan), and fill the baking tray with hot water (really hot tap water will do). The water level should be about halfway up the sides of the springform pan, and make sure that the water doesn't seep through the foil. Place the baking tray in the oven and bake for 60 to 70 minutes, until the cheesecake is set but slightly jiggly in the middle when you shake it gently.

Turn off the oven, and let the cheesecake cool for 15 to 30 minutes while still inside the oven with the oven door left ajar (this way the residual heat helps cook the cheesecake a tad further, plus you don't have to handle the cake while it's too hot).

(continued)

Cherry Pie Brownie Cheesecake (cont.)

Milk Chocolate Ganache

340 g (12 oz) milk chocolate chips

½ cup (118 ml) whipping cream

Pinch of salt

Caramelized Pie Crust Circles

Prepared pie crust dough

1 egg, whisked

Sugar, for sprinkling

Remove the cheesecake from the oven and the water bath, and let cool to room temperature completely; this can take up to 4 hours, depending on the ambient room temperature.

Gently loosen the cheesecake from the pan. If the cheesecake is sticking slightly to the pan, you can run a thin butter knife along the edge of the pan to loosen the cake. Cover the cheesecake and refrigerate for at least 8 hours or overnight.

Chocolate Ganache

Place the chocolate in a heatproof bowl. Add the cream and salt and microwave in 30-second intervals, stirring in between, until the chocolate has melted. Mix to make sure the ganache is smooth and let cool to a thick but pourable consistency.

Caramelized Pie Crust Circles

Preheat the oven to 350°F (180°C). Line a baking sheet with parchment paper.

Roll out the pie crust on a floured surface. Cut out twelve 2- to 3-inch (5- to 8-cm) circles from the pie crust. Place the circles on the prepared baking sheet. Brush the tops with the egg wash and bake until golden brown, 4 to 6 minutes. Remove from the oven, and generously sprinkle the tops with some sugar. Using a blowtorch, melt the sugar to caramelize. Let cool completely and store in an airtight container.

Decorate

Once the cheesecake is chilled, spread the cooled chocolate ganache on the sides. Transfer the remaining chocolate ganache to a pastry bag with an open star tip and pipe 12 swirls on top of the cheesecake. Place a caramelized pie crust circle on top of each chocolate swirl just before serving.

Brownie Bottom Pumpkin Cheesecake

For those who can never decide between pumpkin pie and chocolate on Thanksgiving, this is a chocolate pie in the form of a chocolate brownie layer and pumpkin pie in the form of a creamy pumpkin cheesecake.

Makes one 8–inch (20–cm) cake

Brownie Bottom

115 g (4 oz) bittersweet chocolate

115 g (4 oz) unsalted butter

170 g (6 oz) granulated sugar

¼ tsp salt

1 tsp vanilla extract

2 eggs

94 g (3.3 oz) all-purpose flour

Pumpkin Cheesecake Layer

455 g (16 oz) cream cheese, softened

½ cup (120 g) granulated sugar

200 g (7 oz) pumpkin puree

2 tsp (6 g) cornflour (cornstarch)

Pinch of salt (to enhance flavor, optional)

¼ cup (59 ml) whipping cream

½ tsp pumpkin pie spice

1 tsp vanilla extract

2 eggs

1 egg yolk

Brownie Bottom

Preheat the oven to 350°F (180°C). Butter an 8-inch (20-cm) wide, 3-inch (8-cm) tall springform pan. Line the bottom with parchment paper and dust the sides with flour.

Melt the chocolate and butter in the microwave in 30-second intervals, stirring in between to prevent the chocolate from burning. Let the chocolate-butter mix cool.

When the mixture has cooled, add the granulated sugar, salt and vanilla, and whisk to combine. Next, add the eggs, one at a time, whisking each one well before adding the next. Fold in the flour until just combined.

Pour the batter into the prepared cake pan and bake for 15 minutes. Remove from the oven and let cool for 10 to 15 minutes. Lower the oven temperature to 300°F (150°C) to bake the cheesecake.

Pumpkin Cheesecake Layer

While the brownie layer is baking, get the cheesecake layer ready.

In a bowl using a hand mixer, whip the cream cheese and granulated sugar until creamy and smooth. Add the pumpkin puree, cornflour, salt, cream, pumpkin spice and vanilla and mix on medium speed until the ingredients are well combined and the batter is smooth. Add the eggs and egg yolk, one at a time, and mix on low speed or manually with a balloon whisk until fully incorporated (taking care not to overbeat).

Pour the cheesecake batter over the slightly cooled brownie layer. Tightly double wrap the bottom of your springform pan with two pieces of foil. Then place the springform pan in a larger baking tray (that can easily fit the 8-inch [20-cm] pan), and fill the baking tray with hot water (really hot tap water will do). The water level should be about halfway up the sides of the springform pan, and make sure that the water doesn't seep through the foil. Place the baking tray in the oven and bake for 60 to 70 minutes, until the cheesecake is set but slightly jiggly in the middle when you shake it gently.

Turn off the oven, and let the cheesecake cool for 15 to 30 minutes while still inside the oven with the oven door left ajar (this way the residual heat helps cook the cheesecake a tad further, plus you don't have to handle the cake while it's too hot).

Remove the cheesecake from the oven and the water bath, and let cool to room temperature completely; this can take up to 4 hours, depending on the ambient room temperature.

(continued)

Brownie Bottom
Pumpkin Cheesecake (cont.)

White Chocolate Ganache

200 g (7 oz) white chocolate

¼ cup (59 ml) whipping cream

Mocha Fudge Sauce

⅔ cup (158 ml) whipping cream

3 tbsp (44 ml) corn syrup

1 espresso shot (or 1 heaping tsp instant coffee granules)

50 g (1.7 oz) granulated sugar

70 g (2.5 oz) brown sugar

30 g (1 oz) unsweetened cocoa powder

¼ tsp kosher salt

1 tsp vanilla extract

200 g (7 oz) semisweet chocolate, chopped or chips

2 tbsp (29 g) unsalted butter

Gently loosen the cheesecake from the pan. If the cheesecake is sticking slightly to the pan, you can run a thin butter knife along the edge of the pan to loosen the cake. Cover the cheesecake and refrigerate for at least 8 hours or overnight.

White Chocolate Ganache

Heat the white chocolate and cream together in the microwave in 30-second intervals, stirring in between, until the chocolate has melted. Mix until you have a smooth white chocolate ganache. Let cool until it reaches a spreadable consistency.

Mocha Fudge Sauce

Place the cream, corn syrup, espresso, granulated and brown sugars, cocoa, salt and vanilla in a saucepan over medium-high heat. Whisk the mixture to melt the sugar and cocoa powder, then bring to a boil. Reduce the heat to medium and let it simmer for about 5 minutes. Remove from the heat and stir in the chocolate and butter. Pour the chocolate sauce into a glass jar and let cool completely before using.

Decorate

Once the cheesecake is chilled, use an angled spatula to coat the side of the chilled cheesecake with a thin layer of white chocolate ganache, and coat the top with the mocha fudge sauce. Transfer the remaining ganche to a pastry bag with an open star tip and pipe white chocolate swirls along the top edge. Refrigerate until the ganache and fudge sauce set.

Ginger Brownie
Passion Fruit Cheesecake

Every year, I wait for passion fruit season. I live in the Midwest currently, and passion fruits are precious to me. A fruit that I once used to eat until my stomach ached is near impossible to find where I live now. With its unique combination of citrus, floral and fruity flavors, passion fruits are one of a kind. This tropical passion fruit cheesecake gets a nice kick with fresh ginger in the brownie that takes it to a whole new level.

Makes one 8-inch (20-cm) cake

Chocolate Ginger Brownie

115 g (4 oz) bittersweet chocolate, chopped

115 g (4 oz) unsalted butter

140 g (5 oz) sugar

1 tbsp (14 g) grated fresh ginger

¼ tsp salt

1 tsp vanilla extract

2 eggs

94 g (3.3 oz) all-purpose flour

Passion Fruit Cheesecake

455 g (16 oz) cream cheese, softened

2 tsp (6 g) cornflour (cornstarch)

100 g (3.5 oz) sugar

½ cup (118 ml) fresh passion fruit pulp (5–6 passion fruits depending on the size; frozen and thawed is OK, too)

Pinch of salt

¼ cup (59 ml) whipping cream

1 tsp vanilla extract

2 eggs

1 egg yolk

Chocolate Ginger Brownie

Preheat the oven to 350°F (180°C). Butter an 8-inch (20-cm) wide, 3-inch (8-cm) tall springform pan. Line the bottom with parchment paper and dust the sides with flour.

Melt the chocolate and butter in the microwave in 30-second intervals in the microwave, stirring in between to prevent the chocolate from burning. Let the chocolate-butter mix cool slightly.

When the mixture has cooled, add the sugar, ginger, salt and vanilla, and whisk to combine. Next, add the eggs, one at a time, whisking each one really well before adding the next. Fold in the flour until just combined.

Pour the batter into the prepared cake pan and bake for 15 minutes. Remove from the oven and let cool for 10 to 15 minutes. Lower the oven temperature to 300°F (150°C) to bake the cheesecake.

Passion Fruit Cheesecake

While the brownie layer is baking, get the cheesecake layer ready.

In a bowl using a hand mixer, whip the cream cheese, cornflour and sugar until smooth and creamy. Add the passion fruit pulp, salt, cream and vanilla and mix on medium speed until the ingredients have combined well and the mixture is smooth. Add the eggs and egg yolk, one at a time, and mix on low speed or manually with a balloon whisk until fully incorporated (take care not to overbeat).

Pour the cheesecake batter over the slightly cooled brownie layer. Tightly double wrap the bottom of your springform pan with two pieces of foil. Then place the springform pan in a larger baking tray (that can easily fit the 8-inch [20-cm] pan), and fill the baking tray with hot water (really hot tap water will do). The water level should be about halfway up the sides of the springform pan, and make sure that the water doesn't seep through the foil. Place the baking tray in the oven and bake for 60 to 70 minutes, until the cheesecake is set but slightly jiggly in the middle when you shake it gently.

Turn off the oven, and let the cheesecake cool for 15 to 30 minutes while still inside the oven with the oven door left ajar (this way the residual heat helps cook the cheesecake a tad further, plus you don't have to handle the cake while it's too hot).

(continued)

Ginger Brownie Passion Fruit Cheesecake (cont.)

White Chocolate Ganache

200 g (7 oz) white chocolate chips

½ cup (118 ml) whipping cream

Pinch of salt

Passion Fruit Topping

¾ cup (177 ml) passion fruit pulp

½ cup (96 g) sugar

To Decorate

Crystallized ginger

Remove the cheesecake from the oven and the water bath, and let cool to room temperature completely; this can take up to 4 hours, depending on the ambient room temperature.

Gently loosen the cheesecake from the pan. If the cheesecake is sticking slightly to the pan, you can run a thin butter knife along the edge of the pan to loosen the cake. Cover the cheesecake and refrigerate for at least 8 hours or overnight.

White Chocolate Ganache

Place the white chocolate chips in a heatproof bowl. Add the cream and salt and microwave in 30-second intervals, stirring in between, until the chocolate has melted (white chocolate burns easily, so be careful when heating the ganache). Mix to make sure the ganache is smooth and let cool slightly to a thick but spreadable consistency. As it cools down it will thicken further, but can be heated again to the desired consistency if needed.

Passion Fruit Topping

Place the passion fruit pulp and sugar in a saucepan over medium heat, whisking frequently. Let the liquid simmer for a few minutes, until you have a syrupy consistency.

Decorate

Once the cheesecake is chilled, spread the white chocolate ganache on the sides and top with the passion fruit topping and crystallized ginger.

Brownie Bottom
Candied Bacon Cheesecake

Why would you want to make this cake? One word—bacon. Two words? Candied bacon. The butterscotch cheesecake layer is actually infused with bacon flavor throughout because of the candied bacon studded in the cheesecake. Before you decide bacon in desserts is not for you, consider this—don't we all love pancakes and bacon with pancake syrup? This is a creamier, more indulgent and altogether better version of that! I mean, it's got chocolate, too.

Makes one 8-inch (20-cm) cake

Candied Bacon

8 strips bacon

8 tbsp (110 g) brown sugar

Brownie Bottom

115 g (4 oz) bittersweet chocolate

115 g (4 oz) unsalted butter

142 g (5 oz) granulated sugar

¼ tsp salt

1 tsp vanilla extract

2 eggs

94 g (3.3 oz) all-purpose flour

Candied Bacon Butterscotch Cheesecake

455 g (16 oz) cream cheese, softened

2 tsp (6 g) cornflour (cornstarch)

115 g (4 oz) brown sugar

Pinch of salt

½ cup (118 ml) whipping cream

2 tsp (30 ml) vanilla extract

3 eggs

Candied Bacon

This can be made ahead of time. Preheat the oven to 375°F (190°C).

Place a baking rack over a half sheet pan. Place the bacon strips on the rack and sprinkle the brown sugar on each side of all the bacon strips. Bake for 10 minutes on one side. Flip over the bacon strips and bake for 5 to 10 minutes longer, until the bacon is caramelized (but not burned!).

Remove from the oven. Remove the bacon from the rack, blot them dry with paper towels to remove any excess oil and let them cool completely.

Chop 4 of the bacon strips into small pieces. Set aside (this will be added to the cheesecake batter). Chop the remaining 4 bacon strips into thirds or halves. Set aside (this will be used to decorate the cheesecake).

Brownie Bottom

Preheat the oven to 350°F (180°C). Butter an 8-inch (20-cm) wide, 3-inch (8-cm) tall springform pan. Line the bottom with parchment paper and dust the sides with flour.

Melt the chocolate and butter in the microwave in 30-second intervals, stirring in between to prevent the chocolate from burning. Let the chocolate-butter mix cool.

When the mixture is cool, add the granulated sugar, salt and vanilla and whisk to combine. Next, add the eggs, one at a time, whisking each one really well before adding the next. Fold in the flour until just combined.

Pour the batter into the prepared cake pan and bake for 15 minutes. Remove from the oven and let cool for 10 to 15 minutes. Lower the oven temperature to 300°F (150°C) to bake the cheesecake.

Candied Bacon Butterscotch Cheesecake

While the brownie layer is baking, get the cheesecake layer ready.

In a bowl using a hand mixer, whip the cream cheese, cornflour and brown sugar until creamy and smooth. Add the salt, cream and vanilla and mix on medium speed until the ingredients are well combined and the batter is smooth. Add the eggs, one at a time, and mix on low speed or manually with a balloon whisk until fully incorporated (taking care not to overbeat).

(continued)

Chocolate Ganache

340 g (12 oz) semisweet chocolate, chopped or chips

Pinch of salt

1 cup (236 ml) whipping cream

Pour the cheesecake batter over the slightly cooled brownie layer. Sprinkle the reserved chopped candied bacon over the cheesecake, and swirl the bacon pieces into the batter. Tightly double wrap the bottom of your springform pan with two pieces of foil. Then place the springform pan in a larger baking tray (that can easily fit the 8-inch [20-cm] pan), and fill the baking tray with hot water (really hot tap water will do). The water level should be about halfway up the sides of the springform pan, and make sure that the water doesn't seep through the foil. Place the baking tray in the oven and bake for 60 to 70 minutes, until the cheesecake is set but slightly jiggly in the middle when you shake it gently.

Turn off the oven, and let the cheesecake cool for 15 to 30 minutes while still inside the oven with the oven door left ajar (this way the residual heat helps cook the cheesecake a tad further, plus you don't have to handle the cake while it's too hot).

Remove the cheesecake from the oven and the water bath, and let cool to room temperature completely; this can take up to 4 hours, depending on the ambient room temperature.

Gently loosen the cheesecake from the pan. If the cheesecake is sticking slightly to the pan, you can run a thin butter knife along the edge of the pan to loosen the cake. Cover the cheesecake and refrigerate for at least 8 hours or overnight.

Chocolate Ganache

Melt the chocolate, salt and cream together in a heatproof bowl in 30-second intervals in the microwave, stirring in between to melt the chocolate (take care not to burn it). When the chocolate has melted, let the ganache cool a little (still remaining pourable). If it thickens again, reheat in the microwave for a few more seconds until you have the right consistency.

Decorate

When the cheesecake is chilled, pour half the chocolate ganache on top, letting it drip down the sides. Spread the ganache evenly over the sides. Then let the chocolate ganache set.

Dip half of each of the reserved candied bacon thirds (or halves) in some of the remaining chocolate ganache and place them on parchment paper. Then transfer them to the fridge to let the ganache set. Let the remaining chocolate ganache cool and thicken to a pipeable consistency. Transfer to a pastry bag with an open star tip and pipe decorative swirls on top of the cheesecake, if desired. Decorate with the chocolate-dipped candied bacon.

Neapolitan Cheesecake

This Neapolitan cheesecake will please everybody. It is three classic flavors in one spectacular dessert: fudgy brownie, a super milky vanilla cheesecake, and a light and fluffy strawberry topping. Who wouldn't succumb to that triple threat?

Makes one 8–inch (20–cm) cake

Chocolate Brownie

115 g (4 oz) bittersweet chocolate

115 g (4 oz) unsalted butter

140 g (5 oz) sugar

¼ tsp salt

1 tsp vanilla extract

2 eggs

94 g (3.3 oz) all-purpose flour

Vanilla Milk Cheesecake

225 g (8 oz) cream cheese, softened

225 g (8 oz) mascarpone cheese, softened

2 tsp (6 g) cornflour (cornstarch)

100 g (3.5 oz) sugar

¼ cup (59 ml) whipping cream

Pinch of salt (to enhance flavor, optional)

1 tbsp (15 ml) vanilla bean paste (or seeds scraped from 1 vanilla bean)

3 eggs

Chocolate Brownie

Preheat the oven to 350°F (180°C). Butter an 8-inch (20-cm) wide, 3-inch (8-cm) tall springform pan. Line the bottom with parchment paper and dust the sides with flour.

Melt the chocolate and butter in the microwave in 30-second intervals, stirring in between to prevent the chocolate from burning. Let the chocolate-butter mix cool.

When the mixture is cool, add the sugar, salt and vanilla and whisk to combine. Next, add the eggs, one at a time, whisking each one really well before adding the next. Fold in the flour until just combined.

Pour the batter into the prepared cake pan and bake for 15 minutes. Remove from the oven and let cool for 10 to 15 minutes. Lower the oven temperature to 300°F (150°C) to bake the cheesecake.

Vanilla Milk Cheesecake

While the brownie layer is baking, get the cheesecake layer ready.

In a bowl, using a hand mixer, whip the cream cheese, mascarpone, cornflour and sugar until smooth and creamy. Add the cream, salt and vanilla bean paste and mix on medium speed until the ingredients have combined well and the mixture is smooth. Add the eggs, one at a time, and mix on low speed or manually with a balloon whisk until fully incorporated (taking care not to overbeat).

Pour the cheesecake batter over the slightly cooled brownie layer. Tightly double wrap the bottom of your springform pan with two pieces of foil. Then place the springform pan in a larger baking tray (that can easily fit the 8-inch [20-cm] pan), and fill the baking tray with hot water (really hot tap water will do). The water level should be about halfway up the sides of the springform pan, and make sure that the water doesn't seep through the foil. Place the baking tray in the oven and bake for 60 to 70 minutes, until the cheesecake is set but slightly jiggly in the middle when you shake it gently.

Turn off the oven, and let the cheesecake cool for 15 to 30 minutes while still inside the oven with the oven door left ajar (this way the residual heat helps cook the cheesecake a tad further, plus you don't have to handle the cake while it's too hot).

Remove the cheesecake from the oven and the water bath, and let cool to room temperature completely; this can take up to 4 hours, depending on the ambient room temperature.

Gently loosen the cheesecake from the pan. If the cheesecake is sticking slightly to the pan, you can run a thin butter knife along the edge of the pan to loosen the cake. Cover the cheesecake and refrigerate for at least 8 hours or overnight.

(continued)

Neapolitan Cheesecake (cont.)

Strawberry Topping

6 tbsp (89 ml) water, divided

1 tsp powdered gelatin

455 g (16 oz) strawberries, hulled (fresh or frozen)

150 g (5.3 oz) sugar

2 tbsp (6 g) cornflour (cornstarch)

1 cup (236 ml) chilled whipping cream

Chocolate Ganache

170 g (6 oz) semisweet chocolate chips

½ cup (118 ml) whipping cream

Pinch of salt

Strawberry Topping

Place 3 tablespoons (44 ml) of the water in a small bowl and evenly sprinkle the gelatin over it. Set aside for 10 to 15 minutes to let the gelatin bloom.

Place the strawberries and sugar in a saucepan. Heat over medium heat, stirring frequently to melt the sugar. Bring the mixture to a boil and let it simmer for 20 minutes (less, if using fresh strawberries), until the strawberries have softened and the liquid is syrupy.

Dissolve the cornflour in the remaining 3 tablespoons (44 ml) of hot water. Add this to the strawberry syrup and let it cook for a few more minutes until it has thickened. Remove the saucepan from the heat and add the bloomed gelatin. Whisk to completely dissolve the gelatin in the residual heat. Place the mixture in a bowl to cool.

When the strawberry filling has cooled, prepare the whipped cream. Add the chilled whipping cream to a cold bowl. Whisk with the whisk attachment on your hand mixer on medium speed until you get soft peaks that hold their shape. Fold the whipped cream into the cooled strawberry mixture until just combined.

Spread the strawberry topping evenly over the vanilla cheesecake layer. Refrigerate until set.

Chocolate Ganache

Finely chop the semisweet chocolate and place it in a heatproof bowl. Add the cream and salt and microwave in 30-second intervals, stirring in between, until the chocolate has melted.

Mix to make sure the ganache is smooth and let cool to a thick but spreadable consistency.

Decorate

Once the strawberry topping has set, spread the chocolate ganache over the cake. Let the chocolate ganache set, and serve.

Brownie and Mint Cheesecake

If you like After Eight mints as much as I do (which is a lot), then you will LOVE this cheesecake mashup. Every layer is mixed with that refreshing peppermint flavor and studded with mint candies. A thin layer of mint fondant tops it all off. Really.

Makes one 8–inch (20–cm) cake

Mint Brownie Layer

115 g (4 oz) bittersweet chocolate, chopped

115 g (4 oz) unsalted butter

140 g (5 oz) granulated sugar

¼ tsp salt

1 tsp vanilla extract

2 eggs

94 g (3.3 oz) all-purpose flour

70 g (2.5 oz) mini mint patty candies (about 10), each broken into 4 pieces

Mint Chocolate Chip Cheesecake

455 g (16 oz) cream cheese, softened

2 tsp (6 g) cornflour (cornstarch)

100 g (3.5 oz) granulated sugar

Pinch of salt (to enhance flavor, optional)

½ cup (118 ml) whipping cream

Green food coloring (optional)

2 tsp (10 ml) good-quality peppermint extract

Mint Brownie Layer

Preheat the oven to 350°F (180°C). Butter an 8-inch (20-cm) wide, 3-inch (8-cm) tall springform pan. Line the bottom with parchment paper and dust the sides with flour.

Melt the chocolate and butter in the microwave in 30-second intervals, stirring in between to prevent the chocolate from burning. Let the chocolate-butter mix cool.

When the mixture has cooled, add the granulated sugar, salt and vanilla, and whisk to combine. Next, add the eggs, one at a time, whisking each one well before adding the next.

Fold in the flour and broken mint patty candies until just combined.

Pour the batter into the prepared cake pan and bake for 15 minutes. Remove from the oven and let cool for 10 to 15 minutes. Lower the oven temperature to 300°F (150°C) to bake the cheesecake.

Mint Chocolate Chip Cheesecake

While the brownie layer is baking, get the cheesecake layer ready.

In a bowl using a hand mixer, whip the cream cheese, cornflour and granulated sugar until smooth and creamy. Add the salt, cream, a few drops of green coloring and peppermint extract and mix on medium speed until the ingredients have combined well and the mixture is smooth. Add the eggs and egg yolk, one at a time, and mix on low speed or manually with a balloon whisk until fully incorporated. Add more coloring if needed. Do not overbeat. Fold in the chopped mint chocolate.

Pour the cheesecake batter over the slightly cooled brownie layer. Tightly double wrap the bottom of your springform pan with two pieces of foil. Then place the springform pan in a larger baking tray (that can easily fit the 8-inch [20-cm] pan), and fill the baking tray with hot water (really hot tap water will do). The water level should be about halfway up the sides of the springform pan, and make sure that the water doesn't seep through the foil. Place the baking tray in the oven and bake for 60 to 70 minutes, until the cheesecake is set but slightly jiggly in the middle when you shake it gently.

Turn off the oven, and let the cheesecake cool for 15 to 30 minutes while still inside the oven with the oven door left ajar (this way the residual heat helps cook the cheesecake a tad further, plus you don't have to handle the cake while it's too hot).

(continued)

Brownie and Mint
Cheesecake (cont.)

2 eggs

1 egg yolk

115 g (4 oz) mint chocolate (such as Andes), cut into chips

Chocolate Ganache

340 g (12 oz) semisweet chocolate chips

1 cup (236 ml) whipping cream

Pinch of salt

Mint Fondant

280 g (10 oz) confectioners' sugar

2 tsp (10 ml) peppermint extract

2 tbsp (29 g) unsalted butter, softened

3 tbsp (44 ml) cream, or as needed

To Decorate

Mint chocolate candy, chopped

Remove the cheesecake from the oven and the water bath, and let cool to room temperature completely; this can take up to 4 hours, depending on the ambient room temperature.

Gently loosen the cheesecake from the pan. If the cheesecake is sticking slightly to the pan, you can run a thin butter knife along the edge of the pan to loosen the cake. Cover the cheesecake and refrigerate for at least 8 hours or overnight.

Chocolate Ganache

Place the semisweet chocolate in a heatproof bowl. Add the cream and salt, and microwave in 30-second intervals, stirring in between, until the chocolate has melted. Stir to make sure the ganache is smooth and then let cool to a thick but pourable consistency.

Mint Fondant

Place all the ingredients in a bowl and mix with a spoon or whisk until it forms a smooth dough. It should be spreadable but not runny. If it's too thick, mix in a little cream (1 teaspoon at a time) until you get the right consistency.

Decorate

When the cheesecake has chilled, spread the mint fondant layer on top. You can have this layer as thin or as thick as you prefer. Pour the chocolate ganache over the top of the chilled mint fondant, letting it cover the sides as well.

Decorate the top with the chopped chocolate and a drizzle of chocolate ganache, if desired. Keep the cheesecake chilled until ready to serve.

French Toast
Maple Cheesecake

This cake should come as no surprise to anyone who knows me, given how much I love breakfast and brunch food. This is breakfast for dessert and dessert for breakfast. A deliciously custardy French toast layer is topped with a maple syrup–sweetened cheesecake. All that's missing is a few slices of bacon (Hint: see page 51 for candied bacon cheesecake).

Makes one 8–inch (20–cm) cake

French Toast Layer

226 g (8 oz) stale brioche or challah (about 3 thick slices)

1 cup (236 ml) milk

50 g (1.7 oz) granulated sugar

1 egg

Pinch of nutmeg

1 tsp vanilla extract

¼ tsp ground cinnamon

Pinch of salt

Maple Cheesecake

455 g (16 oz) cream cheese, softened

Pinch of salt

1 tsp vanilla extract

½ tsp ground cinnamon

2 tsp (6 g) cornflour (cornstarch)

¼ cup (59 ml) whipping cream

145 g (5 oz) good-quality maple syrup

2 eggs

1 egg yolk

French Toast Layer

Preheat the oven to 350°F (180°C). Butter an 8-inch (20-cm) wide, 3-inch (8-cm) tall springform pan, line the bottom with parchment paper and dust the sides with flour.

Roughly cut the slices of bread into 1-inch (2.5-cm) squares.

In a large bowl, whisk the milk, granulated sugar, egg, nutmeg, vanilla, cinnamon and salt until well blended. Soak the bread pieces in the milk mixture for 10 to 15 minutes, until the bread is completely saturated.

Spread the saturated bread pieces in a layer on the bottom of the prepared pan. Press down gently to flatten out the layer. Bake for 15 minutes. Remove from the oven and let cool for 10 to 15 minutes. Reduce the oven temperature to 300°F (150°C) to bake the cheesecake.

Maple Cheesecake

While the French toast layer is baking, get the cheesecake layer ready.

In a bowl using a hand mixer, whip the cream cheese, salt, vanilla, cinnamon, cornflour, cream and maple syrup until creamy and smooth. Add the eggs and egg yolk, one at a time, and mix on low speed or manually with a balloon whisk until fully incorporated (but be careful not to overbeat).

Pour the cheesecake batter over the slightly cooled French toast layer. Tightly double wrap the bottom of your springform pan with two pieces of foil. Then place the springform pan in a larger baking tray (that can easily fit the 8-inch [20-cm] pan), and fill the baking tray with hot water (really hot tap water will do). The water level should be about halfway up the sides of the springform pan, and make sure that the water doesn't seep through the foil. Place the baking tray in the oven and bake for 60 to 70 minutes, until the cheesecake is set but slightly jiggly in the middle when you shake it gently.

Turn off the oven, and let the cheesecake cool for 15 to 30 minutes while still inside the oven with the oven door left ajar (this way the residual heat helps cook the cheesecake a tad further, plus you don't have to handle the cake while it's too hot).

Remove the cheesecake from the oven and the water bath, and let cool to room temperature completely; this can take up to 4 hours, depending on the ambient room temperature.

(continued)

French Toast
Maple Cheesecake (cont.)

Cinnamon Whipped Cream

2 tbsp (30 ml) water

¾ tsp powdered gelatin

1 cup (236 ml) plus ½ tbsp (7 ml) chilled whipping cream, divided

¼ tsp ground cinnamon

1 tsp vanilla extract

¼ cup (33 g) confectioners' sugar

To Decorate

Maple syrup

Fresh berries

Gently loosen the cheesecake from the pan. If the cheesecake is sticking slightly to the pan, you can run a thin butter knife along the edge of the pan to loosen the cake. Cover the cheesecake and refrigerate for at least 8 hours or overnight.

Cinnamon Whipped Cream

Place the water in a small bowl and sprinkle the gelatin over it evenly. Set aside for 10 to 15 minutes to let the gelatin bloom.

Microwave the bloomed gelatin in 10-second intervals, stirring in between, until the gelatin dissolves completely (but do not let the gelatin boil).

Add 1 cup (236 ml) of the chilled whipping cream, cinnamon, vanilla and confectioners' sugar to a cold bowl. Whisk with the whisk attachment at medium speed.

Add the remaining ½ tablespoon (7 ml) chilled cream to the hot, dissolved gelatin mix. Add this gradually to the cream that is being whipped (being careful to pour it near the whisk, so that the gelatin gets mixed in with the cream immediately!). Whisk gently until you get soft peaks. Use immediately.

Decorate

When the cheesecake is chilled, top it with the cinnamon whipped cream. Serve with extra maple syrup and fresh berries.

Hazelnut Brownie Nutella Cheesecake

I have very fond memories of Nutella associated with my grandmother. Nutella was her favorite form of chocolate, and I can't help but wonder how much she would have loved a fudgy cheesecake loaded with Nutella flavor. The hazelnut brownie is chock-full of roasted nutty texture, which makes the flavor of Nutella pop even more.

Makes one 8–inch (20–cm) cake

Hazelnut Brownie

226 g (8 oz) unsalted butter

Pinch of salt

226 g (7.5 oz) brown sugar

2 eggs

1 tsp vanilla extract

170 g (6 oz) roasted hazelnuts

114 g (4 oz) all-purpose flour

1 tbsp (7 g) cocoa powder

Nutella Cheesecake

455 g (16 oz) cream cheese, softened

120 g (4.2 oz) granulated sugar

226 g (8 oz) Nutella

2 tsp (6 g) cornflour (cornstarch)

Pinch of salt

1 tsp vanilla extract

¾ cup (177 ml) whipping cream

2 eggs

1 egg yolk

Hazelnut Brownie

Preheat the oven to 350°F (180°C). Butter an 8-inch (20-cm) wide, 3-inch (8-cm) tall springform pan, line the bottom with parchment paper and dust the sides with flour.

Melt the butter, salt and brown sugar in a heatproof bowl in the microwave in 30-second intervals. Stir to form a smooth butter-sugar mix. Set aside to let cool slightly.

When the mixture has cooled, add the eggs, one at a time, and whisk well between each addition. Stir in the vanilla.

Place the hazelnuts in a food processor and pulse until the coarsely chopped.

Sift the flour and cocoa powder together and add to the brownie batter, along with the coarsely ground hazelnuts, and fold in until the flour is fully incorporated.

Pour the batter into your prepared pan and bake for 20 minutes. Remove from the oven and let cool for at least 10 to 15 minutes. Reduce the oven temperature to 300°F (150°C) to bake the cheesecake.

Nutella Cheesecake

While the brownie layer is baking, get the cheesecake layer ready.

In a bowl using a hand mixer, whip the cream cheese and granulated sugar until creamy and smooth. Add the Nutella, cornflour, salt, vanilla and cream and mix on medium speed until the ingredients are well combined and the batter is nice and smooth. Add the eggs and egg yolk, one at a time, and whisk on slow speed or manually with a balloon whisk until fully combined (but be careful not to overbeat).

Pour the mixture over the slightly cooled hazelnut brownie layer. Tightly double wrap the bottom of your springform pan with two pieces of foil. Then place the springform pan in a larger baking tray (that can easily fit the 8-inch [20-cm] pan), and fill the baking tray with hot water (really hot tap water will do). The water level should be about halfway up the sides of the springform pan, and make sure that the water doesn't seep through the foil. Place the baking tray in the oven and bake for 60 to 70 minutes, until the cheesecake is set but slightly jiggly in the middle when you shake it gently.

Turn off the oven, and let the cheesecake cool for 15 to 30 minutes while still inside the oven with the oven door left ajar (this way the residual heat helps cook the cheesecake a tad further, plus you don't have to handle the cake while it's too hot).

(continued)

Hazelnut Brownie
Nutella Cheesecake (cont.)

Nutella Ganache

340 g (12 oz) Nutella

6 tbsp (89 ml) whipping cream

Pinch of salt

To Decorate

8–12 Ferrero Rocher candies

Remove the cheesecake from the oven and the water bath, and let cool to room temperature completely; this can take up to 4 hours, depending on the ambient room temperature.

Gently loosen the cheesecake from the pan. If the cheesecake is sticking slightly to the pan, you can run a thin butter knife along the edge of the pan to loosen the cake. Cover the cheesecake and refrigerate for at least 8 hours or overnight.

Nutella Ganache

Place the Nutella, cream and salt in a heatproof bowl and heat in the microwave in 10-second intervals to melt the Nutella, stirring in between. If you overheat the Nutella, the oil might separate out and not form a smooth ganache.

Decorate

Spread a thin layer of the Nutella ganache on top of the Nutella cheesecake. Put the rest of the Nutella ganache in a piping bag with an open star tip and pipe 8 to 12 swirls on the top of the cheesecake. Top each swirl with a Ferrero Rocher candy.

Double Chocolate
Raspberry Cheesecake

Of all the berries in the world, I personally think that raspberries pair the best with chocolate. With that beautiful chocolate fudge swirl in the cheesecake layer, this cake is decadent and fruity at the same time. And all those fresh raspberries decorating the cheesecake make it look like a bejeweled crown.

Makes one 8-inch (20-cm) cake

Brownie Bottom

115 g (4 oz) bittersweet chocolate, chopped

115 g (4 oz) unsalted butter

140 g (5 oz) sugar

¼ tsp salt

1 tsp vanilla extract

2 eggs

100 g (3.5 oz) all-purpose flour

Chocolate Fudge Swirl

100 g (3 oz) bittersweet chocolate, chopped

3 tbsp (44 ml) cream

Raspberry Cheesecake

455 g (16 oz) cream cheese, softened

2 tsp (6 g) cornflour (cornstarch)

100 g (3.5 oz) sugar

Pinch of salt

¼ cup (59 ml) whipping cream

170 g (6 oz) frozen raspberries, thawed and pureed

1 tsp vanilla extract

2 eggs

1 egg yolk

Brownie Bottom

Preheat the oven to 350°F (180°C). Butter an 8-inch (20-cm) wide, 3-inch (8-cm) tall springform pan. Line the bottom with parchment paper and dust the sides with flour.

Melt the chocolate and butter in the microwave in 30-second intervals, stirring in between to prevent the chocolate from burning. Let the chocolate-butter mix cool.

When the mixture is cool, add the sugar, salt and vanilla, and whisk to combine. Next, add the eggs, one at a time, whisking each one well before adding the next. Fold in the flour until just combined.

Pour the batter into the prepared cake pan and bake for 15 minutes. Remove from the oven and let cool for 10 to 15 minutes. Lower the oven temperature to 300°F (150°C) to bake the cheesecake.

Chocolate Fudge Swirl

While the brownie layer is baking, get the fudge swirl and cheesecake layer ready.

Melt the chocolate and cream in the microwave in 10-second intervals, stirring until the chocolate is smooth. Set aside to let cool slightly.

Raspberry Cheesecake

In a bowl using a hand mixer, whip the cream cheese, cornflour and sugar until creamy and smooth. Add the salt, cream, raspberry puree and vanilla and mix on medium speed until the ingredients are well combined and the batter is smooth. Add the eggs and egg yolk, one at a time, and mix on low speed or manually with a balloon whisk until fully incorporated (make sure not to overbeat).

Dollop the melted and cooled chocolate layer on the cheesecake batter and fold in a few times to create chocolate swirls (do not overmix, because you don't want the chocolate to mix in with the raspberry cheesecake!).

Gently pour the chocolate-swirled cheesecake batter over the cooled brownie layer.

Tightly double wrap the bottom of your springform pan with two pieces of foil. Then place the springform pan in a larger baking tray (that can easily fit the 8-inch [20-cm] pan), and fill the baking tray with hot water (really hot tap water will do). The water level should be about halfway up the sides of the springform pan, and make sure that the water doesn't seep through the foil. Place the baking tray in the oven and bake for 60 to 70 minutes, until the cheesecake is set but slightly jiggly in the middle when you shake it gently.

(continued)

Double Chocolate
Raspberry Cheesecake (cont.)

Chocolate Ganache

340 g (12 oz) semisweet chocolate chips

1 cup (236 ml) whipping cream

Pinch of salt

To Decorate

⅓ cup (74 g) raspberry preserves, slightly warmed

Fresh raspberries

Turn off the oven, and let the cheesecake cool for 15 to 30 minutes while still inside the oven with the oven door left ajar (this way the residual heat helps cook the cheesecake a tad further, plus you don't have to handle the cake while it's too hot).

Remove the cheesecake from the oven and the water bath, and let cool to room temperature completely; this can take up to 4 hours, depending on the ambient room temperature.

Gently loosen the cheesecake from the pan. If the cheesecake is sticking slightly to the pan, you can run a thin butter knife along the edge of the pan to loosen the cake. Cover the cheesecake and refrigerate for at least 8 hours or overnight.

Chocolate Ganache

Place the semisweet chocolate in a heatproof bowl. Add the cream and salt and microwave in 30-second intervals, stirring in between, until the chocolate has melted. Mix to make sure the ganache is smooth. Set aside to cool. As the chocolate cools, it will thicken and become spreadable. If the ganache is too thick to spread, warm it gently in the microwave to get the desired consistency.

Decorate

When the cheesecake has chilled, spread a thin layer of the cooled and thickened chocolate ganache on the sides of the cheesecake. Place the rest of the chocolate ganache in a piping bag with a large open star tip and pipe swirls on top of the cheesecake. Top with the warmed raspberry preserves and fresh raspberries and chill until ready to serve.

Tim Tam Honeycomb Cheesecake

Tim Tam is the unofficial national cookie (biscuit) of Australia. It's also my favorite cookie in the world! So it seemed only natural for me to take it a step further and pair it with another candy I love—honeycomb. This is a honeycomb-flavored cheesecake with a Tim Tam chocolate malt brownie. If only I had known how to make this when I was a little!

Makes one 8–inch (20–cm) cake

Tim Tam Brownie

115 g (4 oz) bittersweet chocolate, chopped

2 tbsp (11 g) malt powder (drinking malt)

115 g (4 oz) unsalted butter

140 g (5 oz) sugar

¼ tsp salt

1 tsp vanilla extract

2 eggs

94 g (3.3 oz) all-purpose flour

115 g (4 oz) Tim Tam cookies, chopped (about 6 cookies)

Honeycomb Cheesecake

455 g (16 oz) cream cheese, softened

¼ cup (59 ml) whipping cream

Pinch of salt

1 tsp vanilla extract

2 tsp (6 g) cornflour (cornstarch)

142 g (5 oz) golden syrup

2 eggs

1 egg yolk

Tim Tam Brownie

Preheat the oven to 350°F (180°C). Butter an 8-inch (20-cm) wide, 3-inch (8-cm) tall springform pan. Line the bottom with parchment paper and dust the sides with flour.

Melt the chocolate, malt powder and butter in the microwave in 30-second intervals, stirring in between to prevent the chocolate from burning. Let the chocolate-butter mix cool.

When the mixture is cool, add the sugar, salt and vanilla, and whisk to combine. Next, add the eggs, one at a time, whisking each one well before adding the next. Fold in the flour and chopped Tim Tams until just combined.

Pour the batter into the prepared cake pan and bake for 15 minutes. Remove from the oven and let cool for 10 to 15 minutes. Lower the oven temperature to 300°F (150°C) to bake the cheesecake.

Honeycomb Cheesecake

While the brownie layer is baking, get the cheesecake layer ready.

In a bowl using a hand mixer, whip the cream cheese, cream, salt, vanilla, cornflour and golden syrup until smooth and creamy. Add the eggs and egg yolk, one at a time, and mix on low speed or manually with a balloon whisk, until fully incorporated (make sure you do not overbeat).

Pour the cheesecake batter over the slightly cooled brownie layer. Tightly double wrap the bottom of your springform pan with two pieces of foil. Then place the springform pan in a larger baking tray (that can easily fit the 8-inch [20-cm] pan), and fill the baking tray with hot water (really hot tap water will do). The water level should be about halfway up the sides of the springform pan, and make sure that the water doesn't seep through the foil. Place the baking tray in the oven and bake for 60 to 70 minutes, until the cheesecake is set but slightly jiggly in the middle when you shake it gently.

Turn off the oven, and let the cheesecake cool for 15 to 30 minutes while still inside the oven with the oven door left ajar (this way the residual heat helps cook the cheesecake a tad further, plus you don't have to handle the cake while it's too hot).

Remove the cheesecake from the oven and the water bath, and let cool to room temperature completely; this can take up to 4 hours, depending on the ambient room temperature.

(continued)

Tim Tam Honeycomb Cheesecake (cont.)

Chocolate Ganache

170 g (6 oz) semisweet chocolate chips

½ cup (118 ml) whipping cream

Pinch of salt

To Decorate

Tim Tam cookies

Chocolate-covered honeycomb candy (such as Crunchie or Violet Crumble bars), chopped

Gently loosen the cheesecake from the pan. If the cheesecake is sticking slightly to the pan, you can run a thin butter knife along the edge of the pan to loosen the cake. Cover the cheesecake and refrigerate for at least 8 hours or overnight.

Chocolate Ganache

Place the semisweet chocolate in a heatproof bowl. Add the cream and salt and microwave in 30-second intervals, stirring in between, until the chocolate has melted. Stir to make sure the ganache is smooth and then let cool to a thick but pourable consistency.

Decorate

Once the cheesecake is chilled, spread the chocolate ganache on the sides of the cheesecake, and stick the Tim Tam cookies on the sides. Place the chopped honeycomb candy on top just before serving.

Brownie Brown Butter Cheesecake

This is a simple brownie cheesecake. However, I added one crucial ingredient to show you how one little change can truly transform a classic dessert. Brown butter is absolutely glorious. Those toasted milk solids in brown butter have an irresistible nutty flavor that elevate anything you incorporate them into.

Makes one 8–inch (20–cm) cake

Brownie Layer

115 g (4 oz) bittersweet chocolate, chopped

115 g (4 oz) unsalted butter

142 g (5 oz) granulated sugar

¼ tsp salt

1 tsp vanilla extract

2 eggs

95 g (3.3 oz) all-purpose flour

Brown Butter Cheesecake

170 g (6 oz) unsalted butter

½ cup (118 ml) whipping cream

455 g (16 oz) cream cheese, softened

2 tsp (6 g) cornflour (cornstarch)

100 g (3.5 oz) granulated sugar

Pinch of salt

2 tsp (10 ml) vanilla extract

3 eggs

Brownie Layer

Preheat the oven to 350°F (180°C). Butter an 8-inch (20-cm) wide, 3-inch (8-cm) tall springform pan. Line the bottom with parchment paper and dust the sides with flour.

Melt the chocolate and butter in the microwave in 30-second intervals, stirring in between to prevent the chocolate from burning. Let the chocolate-butter mix cool.

When the mixture is cool, add the granulated sugar, salt and vanilla, and whisk to combine. Next, add the eggs, one at a time, whisking each one well before adding the next. Fold in the flour until just combined.

Pour the batter into the prepared cake pan and bake for 15 minutes. Remove from the oven and let cool for 10 to 15 minutes. Lower the oven temperature to 300°F (150°C) to bake the cheesecake.

Brown Butter Cheesecake

While the brownie layer is baking, get the cheesecake layer ready.

Heat the butter in a nonstick saucepan over medium-high heat and cook, stirring frequently. The butter will create a foam as it boils. Keep cooking until the foam subsides, and the butter solids start turning golden brown. Remove from the heat and let the butter solids settle at the bottom of the saucepan. Carefully remove as much of the clarified butter as possible, leaving behind only the butter solids. Add the cream to the butter solids and whisk to disperse the butter solids in the cream.

In a bowl using a hand mixer, whip the cream cheese, brown butter cream, cornflour, granulated sugar, salt and vanilla until smooth and creamy. Add the eggs, one at a time, and mix on low speed or manually with a balloon whisk until fully incorporated (taking care not to overbeat).

Pour the cheesecake batter over the slightly cooled brownie layer. Tightly double wrap the bottom of your springform pan with two pieces of foil. Then place the springform pan in a larger baking tray (that can easily fit the 8-inch [20-cm] pan), and fill the baking tray with hot water (really hot tap water will do). The water level should be about halfway up the sides of the springform pan, and make sure that the water doesn't seep through the foil. Place the baking tray in the oven and bake for 60 to 70 minutes, until the cheesecake is set but slightly jiggly in the middle when you shake it gently.

(continued)

Brownie Brown Butter Cheesecake (cont.)

Brown Butter Butterscotch Sauce

115 g (4 oz) unsalted butter

½ tsp kosher salt

115 g (4 oz) brown sugar

½ cup (118 ml) whipping cream

2 tsp (10 ml) vanilla extract

Chocolate Ganache

340 g (12 oz) semisweet chocolate chips

1 cup (236 ml) whipping cream

Pinch of salt

To Decorate

Whipped cream, optional

Turn off the oven, and let the cheesecake cool for 15 to 30 minutes while still inside the oven with the oven door left ajar (this way the residual heat helps cook the cheesecake a tad further, plus you don't have to handle the cake while it's too hot).

Remove the cheesecake from the oven and the water bath, and let cool to room temperature completely; this can take up to 4 hours, depending on the ambient room temperature.

Gently loosen the cheesecake from the pan. If the cheesecake is sticking slightly to the pan, you can run a thin butter knife along the edge of the pan to loosen the cake. Cover the cheesecake and refrigerate for at least 8 hours or overnight.

Brown Butter Butterscotch Sauce

Melt the butter in a saucepan and bring it to a boil. Keep cooking the butter until the solids turn golden brown in color. Add the salt and brown sugar and whisk frequently until the sauce is smooth and the sugar is completely dissolved. Add the cream while whisking, and then reduce the heat to medium. Bring the mixture to a boil and let the sauce boil gently for a 10 to 15 minutes, stirring frequently, until slightly thickened. Stir in the vanilla. Let the butterscotch sauce cool completely before using.

Chocolate Ganache

Place the semisweet chocolate in a heatproof bowl. Add the cream and salt and microwave in 30-second intervals, stirring in between, until the chocolate has melted. Stir to make sure the ganache is smooth. Set aside to let cool. As the chocolate cools, it will become spreadable, and thicken even more as it cools down further. If the ganache is too thick, warm it gently in the microwave to get the desired consistency.

Decorate

Once the cheesecake has chilled, spread a layer of chocolate ganache on the sides of the cheesecake and then a layer of brown butter butterscotch on top. Top with whipped cream, if using. Drizzle with extra brown butterscotch when serving.

Macadamia Brownie White Chocolate Cheesecake with Strawberries

Macadamia and white chocolate are a match made in heaven. The creaminess of each ingredient complements the other. To make it even better, I caramelized the white chocolate, so that it tastes like caramel and dulce de leche. It's a beautifully complex flavor, but it's also easy to make, though it does require some patience. Plus, I'm sharing an easy decorating technique here that you can use on any cake.

Makes one 8–inch (20–cm) cake

Caramelized White Chocolate

226 g (8 oz) good-quality white chocolate

Macadamia Brownie

115 g (4 oz) bittersweet chocolate

115 g (4 oz) unsalted butter

142 g (5 oz) sugar

¼ tsp salt

1 tsp vanilla extract

2 eggs

94 g (3.3 oz) all-purpose flour

115 g (4 oz) macadamia nuts, roughly chopped

Caramelized White Chocolate

This can be done ahead of time. Preheat the oven to 200°F (95°C).

Finely chop the white chocolate. Line a baking tray with a silicone baking mat and spread the chocolate as evenly as possible. Place the baking tray in the oven. Check the chocolate every 10 minutes and, using an offset spatula, mix and re-spread the chocolate as it melts and starts to change color (first it'll be an off-white color and then finally turn light brown, like peanut butter). This can take up to an hour or so, depending on your oven. The chocolate may change texture and become a little chalky, which is why it's important to mix and spread the chocolate as it heats, and even after it comes out of the oven, to keep the chocolate smooth. At this point, the chocolate is ready to be used, or it can be kept in an airtight container. It will harden as it cools, but can be reheated when needed.

Macadamia Brownie

Preheat the oven to 350°F (180°C). Butter an 8-inch (20-cm) wide, 3-inch (8-cm) tall springform pan. Line the bottom with parchment paper and dust the sides with flour.

Melt the chocolate and butter in the microwave in 30-second intervals, stirring in between to prevent the chocolate from burning. Let the chocolate-butter mix cool.

When the mixture is cool, add the sugar, salt and vanilla, and whisk to combine. Next, add the eggs, one at a time, whisking each one well before adding the next. Fold in the flour and macadamia nuts until just combined.

Pour the batter into the prepared cake pan and bake for 15 minutes. Remove from the oven and let cool for 10 to 15 minutes. Lower the oven temperature to 300°F (150°C) to bake the cheesecake.

(continued)

Macadamia Brownie White Chocolate Cheesecake with Strawberries (cont.)

Cheesecake

455 g (16 oz) cream cheese, softened

2 tsp (6 g) cornflour (cornstarch)

⅓ cup (79 ml) whipping cream

½ tsp salt

170 g (6 oz) caramelized white chocolate

2 tsp (10 ml) vanilla extract

3 eggs

White Chocolate Shards

340 g (12 oz) white chocolate, melted

To Decorate

Extra melted white chocolate

Fresh berries

Cheesecake

While the brownie layer is baking, get the cheesecake layer ready.

In a bowl using a hand mixer, whip the cream cheese, cornflour and cream until smooth and creamy. Add the salt, 170 grams (6 oz) caramelized white chocolate and vanilla and mix on medium speed until the ingredients have combined well and the mixture is smooth. Add the eggs, one at a time, and mix on low speed or manually with a balloon whisk until fully incorporated (make sure not to overbeat).

Pour the cheesecake batter over the slightly cooled brownie layer. Tightly double wrap the bottom of your springform pan with two pieces of foil. Then place the springform pan in a larger baking tray (that can easily fit the 8-inch [20-cm] pan), and fill the baking tray with hot water (really hot tap water will do). The water level should be about halfway up the sides of the springform pan, and make sure that the water doesn't seep through the foil. Place the baking tray in the oven and bake for 60 to 70 minutes, until the cheesecake is set but slightly jiggly in the middle when you shake it gently.

Turn off the oven, and let the cheesecake cool for 15 to 30 minutes while still inside the oven with the oven door left ajar (this way the residual heat helps cook the cheesecake a tad further, plus you don't have to handle the cake while it's too hot).

Remove the cheesecake from the oven and the water bath, and let cool to room temperature completely; this can take up to 4 hours, depending on the ambient room temperature.

Gently loosen the cheesecake from the pan. If the cheesecake is sticking slightly to the pan, you can run a thin butter knife along the edge of the pan to loosen the cake. Cover the cheesecake and refrigerate for at least 8 hours or overnight.

White Chocolate Shards

Cut four identical pieces of parchment paper or wax paper at least 4 inches (10 cm) in width (to cover the height of the cake) and 10 to 12 inches (25 to 30 cm) in length (long enough to cover the cake).

Spread the melted chocolate in a thin layer on one piece of parchment or wax paper. Place the other parchment paper over the chocolate and flatten it smooth. Roll up the parchment paper along the long edge and then secure the edges to keep the parchment roll from unraveling. Repeat with the remaining 2 pieces of wax paper. Let the chocolate set. When completely set, unroll the parchment, which will cause the chocolate to break up into curved shards.

Decorate

Once the cheesecake is chilled, use extra melted chocolate to stick the chocolate shards on the sides. Top the cheesecake with fresh berries and serve.

Dessert Mash-Ups

Here, I'm sharing some of my favorite cake and dessert recipes that are either a twist on classics or a mashup of two desserts. I found inspiration from different parts of the world where I have lived.

From everyday entertaining cakes like the Upside-Down Blood Orange and Cardamom Cream Cheese Cake (page 81) to showstopping treats like the Fizzy Pink Champagne and Elderflower Celebration Cake (page 115), each recipe features a secret layer or an element of surprise, making these cakes exciting not only for you, the baker, but also for those who get to enjoy the delicious product of your creativity!

So don't be afraid to be adventurous with these flavors and textures. In the end, you'll be rewarded with cake! That's always a good deal in my opinion.

Upside-Down Blood Orange and Cardamom Cream Cheese Cake

This is without a doubt one of my favorite cakes to make as well as eat—it's sweet, citrusy, light and fudgy all in one! If blood oranges aren't in season, I use oranges or tangerines instead. I especially love the striking color of the cake and the surprise element—the cream cheese layer in the middle.

Makes one 8—inch (20—cm) cake

Blood Orange Layer

115 g (4 oz) unsalted butter

115 g (4 oz) brown sugar

4–5 blood oranges

Cream Cheese Layer

226 g (8 oz) cream cheese

50 g (1.7 oz) granulated sugar

¼ tsp cardamom

¼ cup (59 ml) whipping cream

1 egg yolk

Cardamom Cake

170 g (6 oz) unsalted butter

Zest of 4–5 blood oranges

¼ tsp ground cardamom

¼ tsp salt

212 g (7.5 oz) granulated sugar

3 eggs

¼ cup (59 ml) milk

1 tsp (5 ml) vanilla extract

170 g (6 oz) all-purpose flour

1½ tsp (6 g) baking powder

Confectioners' sugar or whipped cream, to serve

Blood Orange Layer

Preheat the oven to 325°F (165°C). Butter an 8-inch (20-cm) wide, 3-inch (8-cm) tall springform pan. Line the bottom with parchment paper and dust the sides with flour.

Place the butter and brown sugar in a bowl and mix with a spoon until you form a smooth sugar paste. Spread this evenly over the bottom of the pan. Zest the blood oranges and save the zest for the cake. Cut off the remaining rind and slice the blood oranges into ½-inch (1.9-cm) thick slices. Place the orange slices over the butter-sugar layer, letting them overlap a little so that you completely cover the bottom of the pan.

Cream Cheese Layer

Place all the ingredients, except the egg yolk, in a bowl. Mix with a hand mixer until smooth and creamy. Add the yolk and whisk until just combined. Set aside.

Cardamom Cake Layer

In a bowl using a hand mixer, cream the butter, blood orange zest, cardamom, salt and granulated sugar until fluffy. Add the eggs, one at a time, whisking well after each addition. Whisk in the milk and vanilla. Sift the flour and baking powder together, and fold this into the batter in two additions until just mixed through. Pour two-thirds of the batter over the blood orange layer and spread it evenly to cover the blood orange slices. Carefully pour the cream cheese layer on top of the cake layer into the center, taking care not to let it spread all the way to the edges. This helps the cream cheese layer sink while baking.

Dollop the remaining cake batter over the cream cheese layer and spread it evenly to cover the cream cheese. Gently tap the cake pan on the work surface to remove any air trapped inside the batter.

Bake for 60 to 70 minutes, until the cake surface is slightly springy to the touch or a toothpick inserted into the cake comes out clean with only a few crumbs attached. The cake will seem wobbly because of the caramel sauce at the bottom. Remove from the oven and let cool until it's cool enough to handle. Turn the cake out onto a serving tray and let it chill in the fridge overnight, covered. Serve with confectioners' sugar or whipped cream.

Tres Leches
Boston Cream Cake

There's a reason why tres leches cake is so popular. A milk-soaked sweet cake is just so satisfying. But instead of using whipped cream to top my tres leches, I topped this cake with a layer of light, fluffy, custardy pastry cream and a layer of chocolate ganache, making this the sinful union between a Boston cream pie and a tres leches cake.

Makes one 8-inch (20-cm) cake

Vanilla Cake Layer

115 g (4 oz) unsalted butter

½ tsp ground cinnamon

¼ tsp salt

142 g (5 oz) sugar

2 eggs

¼ cup (59 ml) milk

1 tsp vanilla extract

115 g (4 oz) all-purpose flour

1 tsp baking powder

Milk Mix for Soaking the Cake

¼ cup (57 g) sweetened condensed milk

¼ cup (55 g) evaporated milk

¼ cup (59 ml) whipping cream

Pastry Cream Layer

1½ tsp (5 g) powdered gelatin

3 tbsp (44 ml) water

2 eggs

1 tbsp (9 g) cornflour (cornstarch)

1 cup (236 ml) half-and-half (or ½ cup [118 ml] milk and ½ cup [118 ml] cream)

Vanilla Cake Layer

Preheat the oven to 325°F (165°C). Butter and line the bottom of an 8-inch (20-cm) pan with parchment paper and dust the sides with flour.

In a bowl using a hand mixer, cream the butter, cinnamon, salt and sugar until fluffy. Add the eggs, one at a time, whisking well between each addition. Whisk in the milk and vanilla. Sift the flour and baking powder together, and fold it into the batter in two additions just mixed through.

Scrape the batter into the prepared pan and bake for 20 to 25 minutes, until the cake is slightly springy to the touch or a toothpick inserted into the cake comes out clean. Remove from the oven and let cool a bit.

Turn the cake out onto a cooling rack and let cool completely.

Line the bottom of an 8-inch (20-cm) pastry ring or springform pan (you can either use a new pan or the same pan that you used to bake the cake) with parchment paper and line the sides with parchment paper or acetate paper. When the cake has cooled completely, place it in the lined pan.

Milk Mix for Soaking the Cake

Combine the milks and cream in a jug or bowl and whisk together. Pour the liquid over the cooled cake layer (after it has been transferred to the lined springform pan).

Pastry Cream Layer

Sprinkle the gelatin over the water in a bowl and let it bloom for 10 to 15 minutes.

In a bowl, whisk the eggs and cornflour together to form a smooth paste.

Place the half-and-half, sugar and salt in a saucepan and heat to melt the sugar. When the milk is starting to steam, add some of the hot milk to the egg mixture, whisking, to temper the eggs. Add the tempered eggs to the milk and heat the custard over medium heat, stirring continuously to thicken the custard, 6 to 10 minutes. Remove from the heat and add the bloomed gelatin and vanilla. Whisk to dissolve the gelatin completely. Let the custard cool slightly while whisking occasionally.

In a bowl using the whisk attachment on a hand mixer, whisk the cream on medium speed until you have soft peaks. Fold the whipped cream in two additions into the custard until just combined.

Spread the pastry cream layer over the milk-soaked cake layer, making sure the surface is smooth and even. Refrigerate the cake until set.

(continued)

Tres Leches
Boston Cream Cake (cont.)

67 g (2.4 oz) sugar

Pinch of salt

1 tbsp (15 ml) vanilla bean paste

1½ cups (355 ml) whipping cream

Chocolate Ganache

170 g (6 oz) semisweet chocolate chips

½ cup (118 ml) whipping cream

Pinch of salt

To Decorate

8-12 strawberries, patted dry

Chocolate Ganache

Place the semisweet chocolate in a heatproof bowl. Add the cream and salt and microwave in 30-second intervals, stirring in between, until the chocolate has melted. Stir to make sure the ganache is smooth and let cool to a thick but pourable consistency.

Decorate

When the cake has set, remove the cake from the springform pan and remove the acetate paper from around the cake. Pour some of the chocolate ganache in a thin layer over the pastry cream layer on top and on the sides of the cake. Dip the strawberries into the remaining chocolate ganache and place them along the top border of the cake. Refrigerate to set the ganache.

Fudgy Pistachio Baklava Cake

Baklava is legendary around these parts because it's one of my husband's absolute favorite desserts!
I combined pistachio cake with flaky, crispy layers of baklava in this amazingly decadent dessert.
Alternating layers of fudgy filo (almost like a sweeter galaktoboureko) and crispy, flaky filo,
all soaked in a spiced rose syrup, make this baklava cake ridiculously addictive.

Makes one 8—inch (20—cm) cake

Pistachio Cake

90 g (3.2 oz) raw unsalted pistachios

115 g (4 oz) unsalted butter

Pinch of salt

115 g (4 oz) sugar

2 eggs

Zest of 1 orange

½ tsp ground cinnamon

¼ cup (59 ml) milk

1 tsp vanilla extract

71 g (2.5 oz) all-purpose flour

1 tsp baking powder

Nut Layers

285 g (10 oz) nuts (at least one half should be pistachios, and the rest can be walnuts, almonds, etc.)

½ cup (96 g) granulated sugar

½ tsp ground cinnamon

Baklava Layers

226 g (8 oz) filo (20 sheets, 23 x 33 cm [9" x 13"])

170 g (6 oz) unsalted butter, melted

Pistachio Cake

Preheat the oven to 300°F (150°C). Butter and line the bottom of an 8-inch (20-cm) springform pan with parchment paper and dust the sides with flour.

Place the pistachios in a food processor. Process until finely ground.

In a bowl using a hand mixer, cream the butter, salt and sugar until fluffy. Add the eggs, one at a time, whisking well after each addition. Mix in the ground pistachios, orange zest, cinnamon, milk and vanilla. Sift the flour and baking powder together, and fold it into the batter in two additions until just mixed through.

Scrape the batter into the prepared pan. Keep the pan covered while you prepare the baklava layers.

Nut Layers

Place the nuts in a food processor with the sugar and cinnamon. Pulse a few times to coarsely chop the nuts, then transfer to a bowl. Divide the nut mix (coarsely chopped nuts, cinnamon and sugar) into 5 portions, roughly ¾ cup (75 g) per portion.

Baklava Layers

Set up your workstation to prepare the baklava layers—you will need the coarsely chopped nuts in a bowl, the filo pastry covered with a damp cloth, the melted butter with a pastry brush and a pastry mat or working surface to cut and shape the pastry.

Generously brush 1 pastry sheet with the melted butter, and then stick another pastry sheet on top. Repeat three more times, until you get one filo layer comprising 4 sheets. Now place an 8-inch (20-cm) template (like a cake pan) on top of these buttered and stacked sheets and cut carefully around it. Take the scraps and start sticking them evenly on top of the 8-inch (20-cm) circle (using a little melted butter), so that you end up with one stack of roughly 8 sheets of filo. Brush both sides of the 8-sheet filo layer with some melted butter.

Next, scatter ¾ cup (75 g) of the chopped nuts mix on top of the pistachio cake. Place the buttered stack of 8 filo sheets on top of the scattered nuts, and evenly spread another ¾ cup (75 g) of chopped nuts over it.

Repeat with another layer of roughly 8 filo sheets—place this on top of the nuts, and top that layer in turn with another ¾ cup (75 g) of chopped nuts.

(continued)

Fudgy Pistachio Baklava Cake (cont.)

Spiced Rose Syrup

150 g (5.3 oz) sugar

¼ cup (85 g) honey

½ cup (118 ml) water

2 strips orange zest

¼ tsp ground Ceylon cinnamon

Pinch of salt

1 tbsp (15 ml) rose water

To Decorate

Chopped nuts

Edible rose petals

Confectioners' sugar (optional)

Repeat this process three more times until you end up with 5 layers of flaky filo (each layer consisting of roughly 8 filo sheets) and 5 layers of chopped nuts (ending with a filo layer).

Liberally brush the top of the last filo layer with butter. Using a sharp knife, score the filo layers from the top into 8 wedges (it's important that you do not cut all the way to the edge when scoring).

Bake in the oven for 50 to 60 minutes, until a cake tester inserted into the center of the cake comes out with only a few crumbs and the filo layers are golden brown. In the last 30 minutes of baking time, start preparing the sugar syrup.

Spiced Rose Syrup

Place all the ingredients in a saucepan, and heat over medium-high heat while stirring frequently to melt the sugar. Bring the sugar syrup to a boil and then lower the heat to a simmer.

Simmer the mixture for 15 to 20 minutes, until syrupy. Keep warm until the cake is ready.

Decorate

When the cake is finished baking, remove it from the oven and place the cake pan on a baking tray. Pour the hot syrup evenly over the baklava layers and let the cake soak up that gorgeous spiced rose syrup. Then let the cake cool further in the cake pan, about 4 hours. Once the cake has cooled, remove it from the cake pan. Top it with extra chopped nuts and rose petals (optional) and serve as is or dust it with some confectioners' sugar, if desired.

S'mores Brownie Pie

The graham cracker crust is treated to a beautiful caramel coating here, making it even more crunchy and addictive. The crust is then topped with a fudgy double chocolate brownie and a marshmallowy meringue top. I bet you've never done s'mores like this before!

Makes one 8-inch (20-cm) cake

Salted Butterscotch Graham Cracker Crust

115 g (4 oz) unsalted butter

½ tsp kosher salt

115 g (4 oz) brown sugar

142 g (5 oz) graham crackers (14–16 squares)

42 g (1.5 oz) unsalted butter, melted

Fudgy Brownie Filling

170 g (6 oz) bittersweet chocolate

170 g (6 oz) unsalted butter

212 g (7.5 oz) granulated sugar

¼ tsp salt

1 tsp vanilla extract

3 eggs

115 g (4 oz) semisweet chocolate chips

115 g (4 oz) all-purpose flour

Salted Butterscotch Graham Cracker Crust

Preheat the oven to 350°F (180°C). Line a 9 x 13-inch (23 x 33-cm) sheet pan with parchment paper. Butter an 8-inch (20-cm) wide, 3-inch (8-cm) tall springform pan, line the bottom of the pan with parchment paper and dust the sides with flour.

Melt the butter, salt and brown sugar in a saucepan over medium heat. Whisk to form a smooth butter-sugar mix. Let the mix come to a boil and let it boil for 2 to 3 minutes.

Place the graham crackers in one layer to fit the prepared sheet pan. Pour the hot butter-sugar mix evenly over the crackers (you can use a spatula to spread it). Transfer to the oven and bake for 10 minutes, until you see bubbling along the edges of the pan. Remove from the oven and let cool completely until the toffee hardens.

Break the butterscotch graham crackers into squares. Place the crackers in a food processor and process into fine crumbs. Add the melted butter to the graham cracker crumbs and pulse to mix.

Press the crumb mixture into the bottom of the springform pan to form a crust. Freeze for 30 to 60 minutes to let the crust harden.

Fudgy Brownie Layer

Preheat the oven to 350°F (180°C).

Melt the bittersweet chocolate and butter in the microwave in 30-second intervals, stirring in between to prevent the chocolate from burning. Let the chocolate-butter mix cool. Add the sugar, salt and vanilla, and whisk to combine. Next, add the eggs, one egg at a time, whisking each one really well before adding the next. Fold in the chocolate chips and flour until just combined.

Pour the batter into the pan, on top of the frozen butterscotch graham cracker crust and bake the brownie layer in the oven for 20 minutes. The brownie layer should still be fudgy and soft in the middle. Remove from the oven and let cool to room temperature, about 4 hours depending on the ambient temperature.

Gently remove from the springform pan and chill the cake in the fridge, covered, for at least 8 hours or overnight.

(continued)

Meringue Topping

3 egg whites, at room temperature

150 g (5.3 oz) granulated sugar

Pinch of salt

Pinch of cream of tartar

1 tsp vanilla extract

To Decorate

Chocolate sauce (optional)

Meringue Layer

Make the meringue topping just before serving the s'mores pie.

Bring a little water to a boil in a saucepan. Lower the heat to bring it to a simmer.

Combine the egg whites, sugar, salt and cream of tartar in a clean, dry metal bowl. Place the metal bowl over the simmering water (be careful not to let the water mix with your egg whites), and whisk continuously to dissolve the sugar in the egg whites, 5 to 10 minutes. (You can check if the sugar has dissolved by rubbing some of the egg whites between your fingers—if the sugar has dissolved the egg whites will be smooth; if it feels gritty, it's not there yet.)

When the sugar has completely dissolved, remove the egg whites from the double boiler. Using a whisk attachment in your hand mixer or stand mixer, whisk the mixture on high speed until doubled in volume, the egg whites are thick and glossy and the bowl is cool to the touch. Add the vanilla and whisk in for 1 minute. The meringue is now ready to be used immediately.

Decorate

Pile the meringue on top of the brownie (or pipe the meringue on top), and use a blowtorch to caramelize the meringue. Alternatively, turn on your broiler and broil the meringue for a few minutes until the surface caramelizes. Serve immediately with chocolate sauce, if desired.

Basil Berry Eton Mess Cake

Eton mess was one of the simplest desserts that I loved to make and eat as a kid. I didn't quite like meringues when I was little, but crush the meringue and mix it with some whipped cream and fruits? I was all over that! A raspberry-studded vanilla cake topped with sweet, crunchy berry-swirled cream—this cake is simple, elegant and delicious.

Makes one 8–inch (20–cm) cake

Meringues

200 g (7 oz) granulated sugar

1 tbsp (9 g) cornflour (cornstarch)

4 large egg whites, at room temperature

Pinch of cream of tartar

Pinch of salt

2 tsp (10 ml) vanilla extract

A few drops of gel food coloring (optional)

Vanilla Raspberry Cake Layer

115 g (4 oz) unsalted butter

¼ tsp salt

142 g (5 oz) granulated sugar

2 eggs

½ cup (118 ml) milk

2 tsp vanilla extract

115 g (4 oz) all-purpose flour

1 tsp baking powder

57 g (2 oz) fresh raspberries

Meringues

Preheat the oven to 250°F (120°C). Line a baking sheet with parchment paper.

In a dry food processor, process the granulated sugar until you have superfine sugar granules. Add the cornflour and mix to combine.

Place the egg whites in a clean, dry metal bowl of your stand mixer (you can use a hand mixer or a stand mixer for this, but it'll be easier in a stand mixer). Add the cream of tartar and salt. Whisk on high speed until you have soft peaks. Lower the speed to medium, and gradually add the superfine sugar while continuously whisking the egg whites. Once all the sugar has been added, scrape down the sides of the bowl to get any sugar that may have stuck to the sides. Whisk the egg whites on medium-high speed for another 5–7 minutes, until all the sugar crystals have completely dissolved. (You can check if the sugar has dissolved by rubbing some of the egg whites between your fingers every couple of minutes—if the sugar has dissolved the egg whites will feel smooth; if it feels gritty, the meringue is not ready yet.)

As soon as the sugar has dissolved, add the vanilla and whisk for a few seconds to combine. Add a few drops of coloring and fold in the color to create colored swirls, if desired.

Place dollops of meringue on the prepared pan; you should get about 10 to 12 meringues. Bake in the oven for 2 hours. Turn off the oven and let the meringues cool completely inside the oven (at least 2 hours) with the oven door left ajar.

The meringues can be kept in an airtight container until needed.

Vanilla Raspberry Cake Layer

Preheat the oven to 325°F (165°C). Butter and line the bottom of an 8-inch (20-cm) pan with parchment paper and dust the sides with flour.

Cream the butter, salt and granulated sugar until fluffy. Add the eggs, one at a time, whisking well after each addition. Whisk in the milk and vanilla. Sift the flour and baking powder together, and fold it into the batter in two additions until just mixed through.

Pour the batter into the prepared pan, and stud the cake with the raspberries. Bake for 20 to 25 minutes, until the cake is slightly springy to the touch or a toothpick inserted into the center comes out clean. Remove from the oven and let cool slightly so it's easier to handle. Turn the cake out onto a cooling rack and let cool completely.

Line the sides of an 8-inch (20-cm) springform pan with parchment paper or acetate paper. When the cake has cooled completely, place it in the pan.

(continued)

Cream Filling

¼ cup (59 ml) water

2 tsp (6 g) powdered gelatin

2 cups (473 ml) plus 1 tbsp (15 ml) chilled whipping cream, divided

½ cup (65 g) confectioners' sugar

2 tsp (10 ml) vanilla extract

Berry Swirl

115 g (4 oz) fresh strawberries, sliced

115 g (4 oz) fresh raspberries

115 g (4 oz) blackberries

2 tbsp (24 g) granulated sugar

10–12 basil leaves, thinly sliced

White Chocolate Ganache

400 g (14 oz) white chocolate

¾ cup (177 ml) whipping cream

Pinch of salt

To Decorate

Extra fresh berries

Extra thinly sliced basil leaves

Cream Filling

Place the water in a small bowl and evenly sprinkle the gelatin over it. Set aside for 10 to 15 minutes to let the gelatin bloom.

Microwave the bloomed gelatin in 10-second intervals, stirring in between, until the gelatin is completely dissolved (make sure not to let the gelatin boil).

Add 2 cups (473 ml) of the chilled whipping cream and the confectioners' sugar to a cold bowl. Whisk with the whisk attachment of your hand mixer on medium speed. Add the remaining 1 tablespoon (15 ml) of chilled cream to the hot, dissolved gelatin mix. Add this gradually to the cream that is being whipped (being careful to pour it near the whisk, so that the gelatin gets mixed in with the cream immediately!). Add the vanilla. Whisk gently until you get soft peaks.

Berry Swirl

Place all the berries in a bowl and sprinkle the granulated sugar over the berries. Let the berries macerate for a few hours in the fridge (overnight is fine, too). Add the basil and stir to combine.

Gently mash up about one-fourth of the berries using a fork. Strain the berries into a bowl to separate the berries from the juices.

White Chocolate Ganache

Heat the white chocolate, cream and salt in the microwave in 30-second intervals, stirring in between, until the chocolate chips have melted. Mix until you have a smooth white chocolate ganache. Let cool until it reaches a pourable consistency and is at room temperature.

Decorate

Fold the berry swirl into the cream.

Crush the meringues into pieces and set two-thirds of this aside in an airtight container. Fold one-fourth to one-third of the crushed meringues into the berry and cream mix. Spread the berry cream meringue layer over the cake layer in the pan. Let the cake set in the refrigerator until you're ready to serve (within a few hours, as the meringue pieces will melt inside the cream layer).

Remove the cake from the springform pan and remove the acetate paper from around the cake. Pour the white chocolate ganache on top. Let the ganache drip down the sides of the cake and decorate the cake with more fresh berries, white chocolate ganache swirls, basil leaves and the reserved crushed meringue.

Tiramisu Meringue Cake

I still remember my first tiramisu very fondly. I loved it so much that I was determined
to re-create the recipe at home. Here, I have replaced one of the ladyfinger layers with a crisp,
marshmallowy coffee meringue layer.

Makes one 8–inch (20–cm) cake

Coffee Meringue

100 g (3.5 oz) sugar

½ tbsp (5 g) cornflour
(cornstarch)

2 egg whites, at room
temperature

Pinch of salt

Pinch of cream of tartar

1 tsp instant coffee granules

1 tbsp (15 ml) vodka

Mascarpone Mousse

¼ cup (59 ml) water

1½ tsp (5 g) powdered
gelatin

6 egg yolks

100 g (3.5 oz) sugar

¼ cup (59 ml) Marsala wine

Pinch of salt

455 g (16 oz) mascarpone
cheese, softened

1 cup (236 ml) chilled
whipping cream

Coffee Meringue

Preheat the oven to 250°F (120°C). Line a baking tray with parchment paper and draw one
7-inch (18-cm) circle on it. Turn the parchment paper over, so that the drawn circle is facing
the bottom but you can still see the marking through the paper.

In a dry food processor, process the sugar until you have superfine sugar granules. Add the
cornflour and mix to combine.

You can use a hand mixer or a stand mixer for the next step, but it'll be easier in a stand
mixer. Place the egg whites in a clean, dry metal bowl. Add the salt and cream of tartar.
Whisk on high speed until you have soft peaks. Lower the speed to medium or medium-
high. Start adding the sugar-cornflour mixture slowly and gradually, until all of the sugar has
been added. Stop the mixer and scrape down the sides of the bowl. Whisk continuously on
medium speed until the sugar is completely dissolved, 5 to 7 minutes. (You can check if the
sugar has dissolved by rubbing some of the egg whites between your fingers every couple
of minutes—if the sugar has dissolved, the egg whites will feel smooth; if it feels gritty, the
meringue is not ready yet.)

While the meringue is being whisked, dissolve the coffee granules in the vodka. As soon
as the sugar has dissolved in the meringue, fold in the coffee-vodka mixture to combine.
Spread the meringue evenly inside the marked 7-inch (18-cm) circle.

Bake for about 2 hours, until the meringue is crispy and dry. Turn off the oven, leave the
door ajar and let the meringue cool completely (at least 2 hours).

Mascarpone Mousse

Place the water in a small bowl and sprinkle the gelatin over the surface. Set aside to bloom
for 10 to 15 minutes.

Whisk the egg yolks, sugar, Marsala wine and salt in a metal or heatproof bowl, using a hand
mixer. Whisk until the egg yolks are thick and pale in color.

Bring some water to a boil in a saucepan over medium-high heat. Lower the heat to a simmer,
and place the egg yolk mixture over the simmering water and whisk continuously until the
mixture has thickened and tripled in volume, 10 to 15 minutes. You can use a balloon whisk or
your hand mixer for this (I use a hand mixer, because it's easier).

When the egg yolk mixture has thickened, add the bloomed gelatin and whisk until the
gelatin is completely dissolved. Remove from the double boiler and whisk occasionally until
the mixture has cooled to room temperature.

Add mascarpone cheese to the bowl and mix on low speed until well combined.

In a separate bowl, whisk the chilled cream until you have stiff peaks. Fold the cream into
the mascarpone mixture to combine.

(continued)

Ladyfinger Layer

¼ cup (48 g) sugar

1 cup (236 ml) strong brewed coffee

¼ cup (59 ml) Marsala wine (optional)

10–12 Savoiardi ladyfingers

To Decorate

Cocoa powder

Ladyfinger Layer

Line the bottom of a springform pan with parchment paper and line the sides with parchment or acetate paper. Place the meringue disk at the bottom. Top it with half of the mascarpone mousse.

Dissolve the sugar in the hot coffee. Mix in the Marsala, if using. Soak the ladyfingers (one at a time) in the coffee, about 1 to 2 seconds per side. Place the soaked ladyfingers on top of the mousse in an even layer (you may need to break off pieces to fill in the gaps). Top with the rest of the mascarpone mousse.

Decorate

Chill the cake for a few hours. Unmold the cake gently and remove the acetate paper from around the cake. Dust the cake with cocoa powder and serve (meringue cakes are best eaten within 24 hours, to prevent the meringue from getting too soggy).

Ceylon Cinnamon
Chocolate Meringue Cake

Meringue cakes have always been very popular in my family and they made appearances in many family functions and get-togethers. They look like a regular cake from the outside, but then you cut into it and find light and crisp meringue layers instead. This meringue cake is spiced with Ceylon cinnamon, which is near and dear to me. Ceylon (Sri Lanka) is where I was born, and Ceylon cinnamon (also known as true cinnamon) is the real deal. It adds a delicate, floral, earthy aroma and taste. However, it is more expensive and harder to find (unless you come over to my place, I've got tons of it!), so you can substitute it with regular cinnamon if you can't get your hands on some of that Ceylon stuff.

Makes one 8–inch (20–cm) cake

Ceylon Cinnamon Meringue

200 g (7 oz) granulated sugar

1 tbsp (9 g) cornflour (cornstarch)

4 egg whites, at room temperature

Pinch of cream of tartar

Pinch of salt

1 tsp vanilla extract

½ tbsp (4 g) ground Ceylon cinnamon

Easy Cashew Praline

1 cup (120 g) chopped cashews

115 g (4 oz) unsalted butter

115 g (4 oz) brown sugar

¼ tsp salt

Ceylon Cinnamon Meringue

Preheat the oven to 250°F (120°C). Line a baking tray with parchment paper and draw two 7-inch (18-cm) circles on it. Turn the parchment paper over, so that the drawn circles are facing the bottom but you can still see the lines through the paper.

In a dry food processor, process the sugar until you have superfine sugar granules. Add the cornflour and mix to combine.

Place the egg whites in a clean, dry metal bowl or the bowl of your stand mixer (you can use a hand mixer or a stand mixer for this, but it'll be easier in a stand mixer). Add the cream of tartar and salt. Whisk on high speed until you have soft peaks. Lower speed to medium, and gradually add the sugar while continuously whisking the egg whites. Once all the sugar has been added, scrape down the sides of the bowl to get any sugar that may have stuck to the sides. Whisk the egg whites on medium-high speed for another 5 to 7 minutes, until all the sugar crystals have completely dissolved. (You can check if the sugar has dissolved by rubbing some of the egg whites between your fingers every couple of minutes—if the sugar has dissolved, the egg whites will feel smooth; if it feels gritty, the meringue is not ready yet.) As soon as the sugar has dissolved, add the vanilla and cinnamon and whisk for a few seconds to combine.

Divide the meringue between the two drawn circles and spread it evenly to fill each circle. Bake for 1½ to 2 hours, until the meringue layers are dry.

Turn off the oven and let the meringues cool completely inside the oven, with the oven door left ajar. The meringues can be kept in an airtight container until needed.

Easy Cashew Praline

Preheat the oven to 350°F (180°C). Line a quarter sheet pan with parchment paper and spread the cashews in one layer.

Melt the butter, brown sugar and salt in a saucepan over medium-high heat. Whisk to melt the sugar and create a smooth sauce. Bring the sauce to a boil, and then let it boil for 3 to 4 minutes.

Pour the sauce over the cashews and bake in the oven for 10 minutes (the caramel will be bubbly and dark around the edges, but not burned). Let cool completely and then break up the praline into pieces. Store in an airtight container.

(continued)

Ceylon Cinnamon Chocolate Meringue Cake (cont.)

Chocolate French Buttercream

4 egg yolks

2 eggs

200 g (7 oz) granulated sugar

¼ tsp salt

455 g (16 oz) unsalted butter, softened

170 g (6 oz) bittersweet chocolate, melted and cooled

2 tsp (10 ml) vanilla extract

Chocolate French Buttercream

Place the egg yolks, eggs and granulated sugar in a metal stand mixer bowl. Using a hand mixer, whisk the eggs and sugar until pale and frothy.

Bring some water to a boil in a saucepan. Lower the heat to a simmer. Place the metal bowl over the simmering water and whisk continuously until the sugar has completely melted in the egg yolks.

If you'd like to pasteurize the eggs, bring the temperature of the egg-sugar mix to 150°F (66°C) on a candy thermometer and retain the heat at this temperature for 10 minutes, whisking continuously so that the eggs don't cook and harden.

Remove the bowl from the simmering water and return it to the stand mixer with the whisk attachment (you can continue to use a hand mixer if you prefer). Add the salt and whisk on medium speed until the bowl is cool to the touch (this is important—or it'll be too hot for the butter).

Add the softened butter 1 to 2 tablespoons (14 to 29 g) at a time, whisking well between each addition. The frosting will appear runny and broken, but keep adding all of the butter and it'll become smooth and creamy. Add the cooled, melted bittersweet chocolate and vanilla and whisk until completely combined. Keep the frosting covered until needed. Mix with a spatula to make it smooth just before using.

Decorate

Place a meringue layer on a cake tray (use a little frosting to help it stick to the plate). Add roughly ¾ to 1 cup (170 to 226 g) of frosting and spread it evenly. Top with the second layer of meringue and another layer of frosting. Frost the sides of the cake as well. Smooth the sides to create clean lines, or keep it rustic. Decorate the cake as desired (pipe borders or create a rustic frosting swirl). Top with the cashew praline just before serving. Loosely cover the cake and refrigerate overnight (it's best eaten within 24 hours). The meringue layers are very crisp and prone to cracking, so use a serrated knife to cut into the cake. It is completely normal for there to be some cracking—it's all part of the charm of this cake.

Chocolate Passion Fruit Merveilleux Cake

True to its name, this cake is marvelous! While this particular version is not a true merveilleux cake because it has a chocolate cake layer, the chocolate cake actually adds a nice balance to the creamy, fruity, crisp layers in the cake. And instead of using regular whipped cream, I flavored the whipped cream with fruity, tangy passion fruit! This cake is best eaten within 24 hours. If you can find bottled passion fruit syrup, use 1 cup (236 ml) of it instead of the passion fruit syrup.

Makes one 8—inch (20—cm) cake

Chocolate Cake Layer

142 g (5 oz) granulated sugar

115 g (4 oz) unsalted butter

¼ tsp salt

2 eggs

½ cup (118 ml) milk

1 tsp vanilla extract

85 g (3 oz) all-purpose flour

30 g (1 oz) cocoa powder

1 tsp baking powder

Meringue Layers

100 g (3.5 oz) granulated sugar

½ tbsp (5 g) cornflour (cornstarch)

2 egg whites, at room temperature

Pinch of salt

Pinch of cream of tartar

1 tsp vanilla extract

Chocolate Cake

Preheat the oven to 325°F (165°C). Butter and line the bottom of an 8-inch (20-cm) pan with parchment paper and dust the sides with flour.

In a bowl using a hand mixer, cream the butter, salt and sugar until fluffy. Add the eggs, one at a time, whisking well after each addition. Whisk in the milk and vanilla. Sift the flour, cocoa powder and baking powder together, and fold it into the batter in two additions until just mixed through.

Scrape the batter into the prepared pan, and bake for 20 to 25 minutes, until the cake is slightly springy to the touch or a toothpick inserted into the center comes out clean.

Remove from the oven and let cool slightly. Then turn the cake out onto a cooling rack and let cool completely.

Meringue Layers

Preheat the oven to 250°F (120°C). Line a baking tray with parchment paper and draw two 7-inch (18-cm) circles on it. Turn the parchment paper over, so that the drawn circles are facing the bottom but you can still see the markings through the paper.

In a dry food processor, process the granulated sugar until you have superfine sugar granules. Add the cornflour and mix to combine.

You can use a hand mixer or a stand mixer for this step, but it'll be easier in a stand mixer. Place the egg whites in a clean, dry metal bowl. Add the salt and cream of tartar and whisk on high speed until you have soft peaks. Lower the speed to medium. Start adding the sugar-cornflour mix slowly and gradually, until all of the sugar has been added. Stop the mixer and scrape down the sides of the bowl. Whisk the egg whites on medium-high speed for another 5 to 7 minutes, only until all the sugar crystals have completely dissolved. (You can check if the sugar has dissolved by rubbing some of the egg whites between your fingers every couple of minutes—if the sugar has dissolved, the egg whites will feel smooth; if it feels gritty, the meringue is not ready yet.) Add the vanilla and whisk for a few seconds just to mix in the vanilla.

Divide the meringue between the two 7-inch (18-cm) circles. Spread it evenly inside each drawn circle to fill. Bake for 90 minutes. Turn off the oven, leave the door ajar and let the meringue cool completely. Store in an airtight container until ready to use.

(continued)

Chocolate Passion Fruit Merveilleux Cake (cont.)

Passion Fruit Cream

⅓ cup (79 ml) water

2½ tsp (8 g) powdered gelatin

3 cups (710 ml) plus 1 tbsp (15 ml) chilled whipping cream, divided

1 cup (130 g) confectioners' sugar

2½ tbsp (30 g) powdered freeze-dried passion fruit

Passion Fruit Syrup

¼ cup (59 ml) water

1½ tsp (7 g) powdered gelatin

¾ cup (177 ml) passion fruit pulp (about 10 passion fruits)

½ cup (96 g) granulated sugar

To Decorate

226 g (8 oz) shaved chocolate

Passion Fruit Cream

Place the water in a small bowl and evenly sprinkle the gelatin over it. Set aside for 10 to 15 minutes to let the gelatin bloom. Microwave the bloomed gelatin in 10-second intervals, stirring in between, until the gelatin is completely dissolved (take care not to let the gelatin boil).

Add 3 cups (710 ml) of the chilled whipping cream and confectioners' sugar to a cold bowl. Whisk with the whisk attachment of your hand mixer on medium speed. Add the remaining 1 tablespoon (15 ml) of chilled cream to the hot, dissolved gelatin mix. Add this gradually to the cream that is being whipped (being careful to pour it near the whisk, so that the gelatin gets mixed in with the cream immediately!). Add the passion fruit powder and mix well. Keep whisking on medium speed until you get soft peaks that hold shape. Use immediately.

Passion Fruit Syrup

This can be made the day you serve the cake. Place the water in a small bowl and evenly sprinkle the gelatin over it. Set aside for 10 to 15 minutes to let the gelatin bloom.

Place the passion fruit pulp and granulated sugar in a saucepan over medium heat and whisk to dissolve the sugar. Heat for a few more minutes for a syrupy consistency. If you are using bottled passion fruit syrup, you will need to heat it.

Remove the passion fruit syrup from the heat and add the bloomed gelatin, whisking to dissolve the gelatin. Set aside to cool.

Decorate

Line the bottom of an 8-inch (20-cm) springform pan with parchment paper, and line the sides with parchment paper or acetate paper.

Place the chocolate cake layer at the bottom, followed by one-third of the passion fruit cream. Spread the cream evenly to fill the gaps. Next, place one meringue layer and top it with another one-third of the passion fruit cream (make sure the meringue layer is completely covered and the cream fills the edges of the cake). Repeat with the final meringue layer and the rest of the passion fruit cream. Spread evenly to create a flat surface. Place the cake in the freezer to set.

When the cake is set, pour the passion fruit syrup on top and spread it evenly over the surface. Then, let this passion fruit jelly layer set in the freezer as well.

Take the cake out of the freezer a few hours before you plan to serve, to let the cake and cream layers soften. Remove the cake from the springform pan, remove the acetate paper and gently press chocolate shavings onto the sides of the cake (the cream layer). The cake can be stored like this for about 24 hours in the fridge, but it is best eaten immediately.

Pumpkin Spice
Latte Cake

PSL lovers unite. Whether you like pumpkin spice lattes or not, I bet you will love this cake.
It's like a pumpkin spice tiramisu, and a great and easy alternative for pumpkin pie on Thanksgiving.
Or just a decadent way to celebrate autumn!

Makes one 8—inch (20—cm) cake

Coffee Cake

2½ tsp (3 g) instant coffee granules

½ cup (118 ml) milk

115 g (4 oz) unsalted butter

¼ tsp salt

142 g (5 oz) granulated sugar

2 eggs

1 tsp vanilla extract

115 g (4 oz) all-purpose flour

1 tsp baking powder

Pumpkin Mousse

¼ cup (59 ml) water

2 tsp (6 g) powdered gelatin

230 g (8.1 oz) pumpkin puree

100 g (3.5 oz) granulated sugar

1½ tsp (4 g) pumpkin pie spice

226 g (8 oz) cream cheese, softened

1 cup (236 ml) chilled whipping cream

Coffee Cake

Preheat the oven to 325°F (165°C). Butter and line the bottom of an 8-inch (20-cm) pan with parchment paper and dust the sides with flour.

Dissolve the coffee granules in the milk and set aside.

In a bowl using a hand mixer, cream the butter, salt and granulated sugar until fluffy. Add the eggs, one at a time, whisking well after each addition. Whisk in the coffee, milk and vanilla. Sift the flour and baking powder together and fold it into the batter in two additions until just mixed through.

Scrape the batter into the prepared pan and bake for 20 to 25 minutes, until the cake is slightly springy to the touch or a toothpick inserted into the center comes out clean. Remove from the oven and let cool slightly. Turn the cake out onto a cooling rack and let cool completely.

Pumpkin Mousse

Place the water in a small heatproof bowl and sprinkle the gelatin over the surface. Let the gelatin bloom for at least 10 to 15 minutes.

In a saucepan, combine the pumpkin puree, granulated sugar and pumpkin pie spice. Heat over medium heat and stir until the sugar has dissolved and the puree is smooth. Add the bloomed gelatin to the pumpkin and stir to dissolve the gelatin in the residual heat (take care not to let the mixture boil). Remove from the heat as soon as the gelatin has dissolved, transfer to a large bowl and let cool.

When the mixture has cooled, add the softened cream cheese and mix until the cream cheese has no lumps and is mixed smoothly with the pumpkin.

In a separate bowl, whisk the chilled cream until you have soft peaks. Fold the cream into the pumpkin mixture in two additions until just mixed through. Use immediately, before the pumpkin mousse sets.

(continued)

Pumpkin Spice
Latte Cake (cont.)

Stabilized Coffee Whipped Cream

3 tbsp (44 ml) water

1 tsp (3 g) powdered gelatin

1 cup (236 ml) plus ½ tbsp (7 ml) chilled whipping cream, divided

1 tsp instant coffee granules

2 tbsp (30 ml) Kahlúa (optional)

¼ cup (33 g) confectioners' sugar

Ladyfinger Layer

50 g (1.7 oz) granulated sugar

1 cup (118 ml) strong brewed coffee, hot

¼ cup (59 ml) Kahlúa (optional)

12 Savoiardi ladyfingers, plus more to decorate (optional)

Stabilized Coffee Whipped Cream

Place the water in a small bowl and sprinkle the gelatin over the water evenly. Set aside for 10 to 15 minutes to let the gelatin bloom. Microwave the bloomed gelatin in 10-second intervals, stirring in between, until the gelatin dissolves completely (make sure not to let the gelatin boil).

Add 1 cup (236 ml) of the chilled whipping cream, coffee granules, Kahlúa (if using) and confectioners' sugar to a cold bowl. Whisk the cream with the whisk attachment on medium speed. Add the remaining ½ tablespoon (7 ml) of chilled cream to the hot dissolved gelatin mix. Add this gradually to the cream that is being whipped (being careful to pour it near the whisk, so that the gelatin gets mixed in with the cream immediately!). Whisk gently until you get soft peaks and use immediately.

Ladyfinger Layer

When the cake has cooled and the pumpkin spice mousse is ready, line the sides of an 8-inch (20-cm) springform pan with parchment paper or acetate paper and place the cake in the pan.

Dissolve the granulated sugar in the hot coffee. Add the Kahlúa, if using. Brush the surface of the cake with a generous amount of the coffee mixture. Spread half of the mousse on top of the cake.

Soak each ladyfinger in the coffee mix, about 1 to 2 seconds per side (make sure they don't get completely saturated). Cover the mousse layer with these coffee-soaked ladyfingers (you may need to break off a few pieces to fill in the gaps). Top with the rest of the mousse. Let chill in the fridge for a few hours until the mousse has set. When the mousse has set, spread the coffee whipped cream on top and refrigerate until ready to serve.

Remove the cake from the springform pan, and gently remove the parchment or acetate paper. Stick extra ladyfingers on the sides of the cake, if desired, and serve.

Whiskey Mousse Cake

Extra boozy, extra indulgent and extra fun—this is a legit grown-up dessert.

Makes one 8-inch (20-cm) cake

Whiskey–Soaked Brownie Layer

115 g (4 oz) bittersweet chocolate

115 g (4 oz) unsalted butter

¼ tsp salt

142 g (5 oz) sugar

1 tsp vanilla extract

2 eggs

95 g (3.3 oz) all-purpose flour

¼ cup (59 ml) Scotch whiskey

White Chocolate Whiskey Mousse Layer

⅓ cup (79 ml) water

4 tsp (13 g) powdered gelatin

¼ cup (59 ml) whipping cream

6 egg yolks

⅓ cup (79 ml) Scotch whiskey

455 g (16 oz) white chocolate chips (or chopped white chocolate)

2 cups (473 ml) chilled whipping cream

Whiskey–Soaked Brownie Layer

Preheat the oven to 350°F (180°C). Butter an 8-inch (20-cm) wide, 3-inch (8-cm) tall springform pan, line the bottom with parchment paper and flour the sides of the pan.

Place the chocolate and butter in a heatproof bowl and melt in the microwave in 30-second intervals, until nice and smooth. Add the salt, sugar and vanilla and whisk to combine. Let cool to room temperature.

Whisk in the eggs, one at a time, whisking well after each addition. Sift in the flour in two additions and fold the flour into the chocolate mix until well combined.

Spread the brownie batter evenly in the prepared pan and bake for 20 minutes.

Remove from the oven and evenly drizzle the Scotch whiskey over the top of the brownie layer. When the brownie has cooled slightly (cool enough to touch), remove from the springform pan. Now let the brownie cool completely to room temperature.

Line the sides of an 8-inch (20-cm) springform pan or cake ring with parchment paper or acetate paper. Place the cooled brownie layer in the lined pan.

White Chocolate Whiskey Mousse Layer

Place the water in a bowl and sprinkle the gelatin evenly on top. Mix gently to saturate. Let the gelatin bloom for about 5 to 10 minutes.

Add the bloomed gelatin and cream to a small saucepan and heat over medium heat to melt the gelatin completely. This milk mix should be smooth, with no residual gelatin granules (make sure not to let the mixture boil).

In a separate bowl, whisk the egg yolks and Scotch whiskey until frothy and slightly thick.

Melt the white chocolate in a double boiler over simmering water, stirring frequently, until nice and smooth. Add the egg yolk mixture and the gelatin-cream mixture and whisk well. Stir until the chocolate is smooth with no clumps. Set aside to let the chocolate mix cool slightly (but not too cold that the gelatin starts to set).

Whisk the whipping cream in a cold bowl (a metal bowl in the freezer for a few minutes usually does the trick), until you have soft peaks. Gently fold the whipped cream into the white chocolate in 2 to 3 additions, until well incorporated. A few streaks of white chocolate are OK; you don't want to deflate the mousse by overmixing. Spread the white chocolate mousse over the brownie layer in the prepared cake pan and smooth the top. Refrigerate for at least 6 to 8 hours or up to 24 hours.

(continued)

Whiskey Mousse Cake (cont.)

Whiskey Caramel Sauce

200 g (7 oz) sugar

¼ cup (59 ml) water

2 tbsp (30 ml) corn syrup

Pinch of salt

½ cup (118 ml) whipping cream, warmed

3 tbsp (44 ml) Scotch whiskey

To Decorate

12–14 Biscoff cookies or graham crackers, crushed

Whiskey Caramel Sauce

Add the sugar, water, corn syrup and salt to a saucepan and swirl to combine. Heat over medium heat and let the sugar dissolve without stirring the liquid. Let the sugar syrup come to a boil and gradually change color to a dark golden color. Add the warm cream slowly, while whisking to combine, until you get a smooth caramel sauce, 2 to 5 minutes. Stir in the whiskey and cook for 2 to 5 minutes, until you get a nice caramel sauce consistency. Pour into a glass jar and set aside until needed. It will thicken as it cools down.

Decorate

When you're ready to serve, gently release the cake from the springform pan and peel off the parchment paper. Place it on a cooling rack with parchment paper underneath. Pour the caramel sauce to cover the top of the cake and let it drip down the sides. Spread it in a thin layer over the sides (it doesn't have to be neat—no one's judging!). Gently press the crushed cookies onto the sides of the cake. Slice with a warm knife and serve.

Orange Semolina and *White Chocolate* Chai Mousse Cake

I really love the textures of this soft semolina cake with a smooth, creamy, spiced mousse on top. The sweetness from white chocolate is balanced by chai and the subtle citrus flavor of orange.

Makes one 8–inch (20–cm) cake

Orange Semolina Cake

115 g (4 oz) unsalted butter

¼ tsp salt

170 g (6 oz) sugar

3 eggs

Zest of 1 orange

¼ cup (59 ml) orange juice

½ tsp turmeric

115 g (4 oz) fine semolina

1 tsp baking powder

White Chocolate Chai Mousse

4 tsp (13 g) powdered gelatin

⅓ cup (79 ml) water

3 tbsp (43 g) chai powder

2¼ cups (532 ml) chilled whipping cream, divided

Pinch of salt

6 egg yolks

455 g (16 oz) white chocolate chips (or chopped white chocolate)

Orange Semolina Cake

Preheat the oven to 325°F (165°C). Butter and line the bottom of an 8-inch (20-cm) pan with parchment paper and dust the sides with flour.

In a bowl using a hand mixer, cream the butter, salt and sugar until fluffy. Add the eggs, one at a time, whisking well after each addition. Whisk in the zest, orange juice and turmeric. Fold in the semolina and baking powder until just mixed through.

Scrape the batter into the prepared pan and bake for 20 to 25 minutes, until the cake is slightly springy to the touch or a toothpick inserted into the center comes out clean. Remove from the oven and let cool a bit. Turn the cake out onto a cooling rack and let cool completely.

White Chocolate Chai Mousse

Place the water in a bowl and sprinkle the gelatin evenly over the surface; mix gently to saturate. Let the gelatin bloom for 5 to 10 minutes.

Combine the bloomed gelatin, chai powder, ¼ cup (59 ml) of the cream and salt in a small saucepan and heat over medium heat to melt the gelatin completely. Stir until smooth, with no residual gelatin granules (make sure not to let the mixture boil).

In a separate bowl, whisk the egg yolks until frothy and slightly thick.

Melt the white chocolate in a double boiler over simmering water, stirring frequently, until nice and smooth. Add the whisked egg yolks and the gelatin-chai-milk mixture and whisk well, until the mixture is smooth with no clumps. Set aside to let the chocolate cool slightly (but not too cold that the gelatin starts to set).

Whisk the remaining 2 cups (473 ml) of whipping cream in a cold bowl (a metal bowl in the freezer for a few minutes usually does the trick), until you have soft peaks. Gently fold the whipped cream into the white chocolate in 2 to 3 additions, until well incorporated. A few streaks of white chocolate are OK; you don't want to deflate the mousse by overmixing.

(continued)

Orange Semolina and *White Chocolate* Chai Mousse Cake (cont.)

Chocolate Ganache
170 g (6 oz) semisweet chocolate chips

½ cup (118 ml) whipping cream

Pinch of salt

To Decorate
Orange slices

Chocolate Ganache
Place the semisweet chocolate in a heatproof bowl. Add the cream and salt and microwave in 30-second intervals, stirring in between, until the chocolate has melted. Stir to make sure the ganache is smooth and let cool to a thick but pourable consistency.

Decorate
Line the bottom of an 8-inch (20-cm) springform pan with parchment paper and the sides with parchment paper or acetate paper. Once the semolina cake has cooled, place it in the prepared pan.

Spread the white chocolate mousse over the cake and smooth the top. Refrigerate for at least 4 hours and up to 24 hours.

When ready to serve, gently release the cake from the springform pan. Spread a layer of chocolate ganache on the sides of the cake. Decorate the top of the cake with sliced oranges. Let the ganache set. Keep the cake in the fridge until ready to serve.

Cinnamon Dulce de Leche Torta

The first time I had chocotorta, I was hooked. It's the Argentine version of a Sri Lankan classic called chocolate biscuit (cookie) pudding, but with a creamy dulce de leche. I was inspired by two of my favorite Latin American desserts—churros and chocotorta—for this secret-layer cake. It's a cinnamon cake, topped with chocotorta that I made using Oreos (but can be made with any type of chocolate cookie) and studded with churro chips!

Makes one 8—inch (20—cm) cake

Cinnamon Cake Layer

115 g (4 oz) unsalted butter

1 tsp ground cinnamon

142 g (5 oz) sugar

¼ tsp salt

2 eggs

½ cup (118 ml) milk

1 tsp vanilla extract

115 g (4 oz) all-purpose flour

1 tsp baking powder

Dulce de Leche Layer

¼ cup (59 ml) water

1½ tsp (5 g) powdered gelatin

½ cup (118 ml) chilled whipping cream

340 g (12 oz) cream cheese, softened

455 g (16 oz) dulce de leche

Chocolate Ganache

170 g (6 oz) semisweet chocolate chips

½ cup (118 ml) whipping cream

Pinch of salt

Cinnamon Cake Layer

Preheat the oven to 325°F (165°C). Butter and line the bottom of an 8-inch (20-cm) pan with parchment paper and dust the sides with flour.

In a bowl using a hand mixer, cream the butter, cinnamon, sugar and salt until fluffy. Add the eggs, one at a time, whisking well after each addition. Whisk in the milk and vanilla. Sift the all-purpose flour and baking powder together, and fold it into the batter in two additions until just mixed through.

Scrape the batter into the prepared pan, and bake for 20 to 25 minutes, until the cake is slightly springy to the touch or a toothpick inserted into the center comes out clean. Remove from the oven and let cool a bit. Turn the cake out onto a cooling rack and let cool completely.

Line the bottom of an 8-inch (20-cm) pastry ring or springform pan (you can either use a new pan or the same pan that you used to bake the cake) with parchment paper and the sides with parchment paper or acetate paper. When the cake has cooled completely, place it in the lined springform pan.

Dulce de Leche Layer

Place the water in a heatproof bowl. Sprinkle the powdered gelatin over the surface and let the gelatin bloom for 10 to 15 minutes.

In a separate bowl, whip the chilled cream and cream cheese until fluffy and smooth. Add the dulce de leche and whip until you have a smooth mixture.

Melt the bloomed gelatin in the microwave in 10-second intervals until it's completely dissolved. Pour the gelatin in a gentle stream into the dulce de leche while continuously whisking to make sure it mixes well. Use this before it starts to set.

Chocolate Ganache

Place the semisweet chocolate chips in a heatproof bowl. Add the cream and salt and microwave in 30-second intervals, stirring in between, until the chocolate has melted. Stir to make sure the ganache is smooth and let cool to a thick but pourable consistency.

(continued)

Cinnamon Dulce de Leche Torta (cont.)

Churro Chips

½ cup (96 g) sugar

1 tsp ground cinnamon

4–5 mini flour tortillas

½ cup (118 ml) melted butter

To Assemble

396 g (14 oz) Oreo cookies, separated and filling scraped from the middle, or some other type of plain chocolate cookie

1 cup (236 ml) vanilla or chocolate milk, at room temperature

Churro Chips

Preheat the oven to 350°F (180°C). Line a baking sheet with parchment paper.

In a small bowl mix the sugar and cinnamon together and set aside.

Cut the mini tortillas into 4 quarters, and cut each quarter in half again to create 8 tortilla wedges. Brush each tortilla piece with the melted butter on one side and dip it in the cinnamon sugar mix to adhere. Place the tortilla pieces on the baking sheet. Bake for 10 to 15 minutes, or until the tortilla chips are toasted. Remove from the oven and let cool completely.

Assembly

Spread a thin layer of the dulce de leche filling on top of the cinnamon cake.

Soak the Oreo cookies (separated, with no filling) in the vanilla (or chocolate) milk for 3 to 5 seconds (don't let the cookie get completely soggy) and place it on top of the dulce de leche layer. Repeat until you have two layers of cookie halves. (The reason why I'm creating a double layer is that Oreo cookie halves are too thin, so doubling it up will provide a better ratio of cookie to dulce de leche. If you are using a thicker, sturdier chocolate cookie like Chocolina, then one layer is enough.) Cover the cookies with another thin layer of dulce de leche, and another layer of milk-soaked cookies. Repeat these two layers one more time. Then, add the final layer of dulce de leche on top (you will now have four dulce du leche layers and three double cookie layers). Place the cake in the fridge to set overnight.

Once the cake and dulce de leche layers have set, remove the cake from the springform pan. Top the cake with a thin layer of chocolate ganache and stick the churro chips (sugared side facing out) to the sides of the cake. Keep the cake refrigerated until ready to serve.

Fizzy Pink Champagne and Elderflower Celebration Cake

A celebratory cake in every sense, this champagne-flavored cake is paired with elderflower and topped with popping candy bark that pops and fizzles in your mouth. Wow your guests at your next party with this fizzy pink champagne cake!

Makes one 8—inch (20—cm) cake

Pink Champagne Cake

6 egg whites

2 tsp (10 ml) vanilla extract

1 cup (236 ml) pink champagne

250 g (8.8 oz) all-purpose flour

4 tsp (15 g) baking powder

300 g (10.5 oz) granulated sugar

1 tsp salt

170 g (6 oz) unsalted butter, softened

A drop of pale pink food coloring

Elderflower Buttercream

455 g (16 oz) unsalted butter

Pinch of salt

680 g (24 oz) confectioners' sugar

¼ cup (59 ml) elderflower cordial

2-3 tbsp (30-44 ml) whipping cream (optional, as needed)

Pink Champagne Cake

Preheat the oven to 350°F (180°C). Butter and line the bottom of three 8-inch (20-cm) pans with parchment paper and dust the sides with flour.

In a jug or bowl, whisk to combine the egg whites, vanilla and champagne.

In a large bowl using the paddle attachment, whisk the flour, baking powder, granulated sugar and salt to combine. Slice the butter into tablespoon-size portions and add it to the flour. Mix until the flour resembles crumbs, 2 to 3 minutes. Add about two-thirds of the egg white mixture and a drop of pale pink coloring, and mix on medium speed for a minute or two, until you have a smooth batter. Scrape down the sides. Add the rest of the liquid and whisk just long enough to let the liquid fully mix in. Make sure you scrape down the sides to ensure the batter is mixed well (don't overbeat, or you'll end up with a tough cake texture).

Divide the batter among the three prepared pans and bake for 20 to 25 minutes, or until a toothpick inserted into the center of a cake comes out clean. Remove from the oven and let cool a bit. Turn the cakes out onto a cooling rack and let the cakes cool completely.

Elderflower Buttercream

Place the butter and salt in the mixer bowl and whisk until light and fluffy. Add the confectioners' sugar, a portion at a time, and whisk on low speed until combined. Add the elderflower cordial and whisk for a few minutes, until light and fluffy. The frosting is now ready to be used. Add the cream, 1 tablespoon (15 ml) at a time, if you find the frosting too stiff, for a softer, creamier buttercream.

Transfer the frosting to a large pastry bag with a large round pastry tip when you're ready to use.

(continued)

Fizzy Pink Champagne and Elderflower Celebration Cake (cont.)

White Chocolate Popping Candy Bark

226 g (8 oz) white chocolate

¼ cup (58 g) popping candy

Gold leaf (optional)

Glitter (optional)

Luster dust (optional)

Pink sprinkles (optional)

To Decorate

Cocoa butter–coated popping candy (or smaller pieces from the white chocolate popping candy bark)

Pink food coloring

Gold leaf or glitter

White Chocolate Popping Candy Bark

Line a baking sheet with parchment paper.

Melt the white chocolate in a heatproof bowl in the microwave in 10-second intervals, stirring in between, until melted and smooth. Allow the chocolate to cool to 85°F (30°C) on a candy thermometer. Add the popping candy to the chocolate and gently stir. Gently spread the white chocolate on the parchment paper as thin as you can without damaging the popping candy. Sprinkle with the gold leaf, glitter, luster dust or pink sprinkles, if desired. Let the chocolate set completely (in the fridge or freezer) and then chop a few into smaller pieces to mix with the buttercream.

Decorate

Place one cake layer on a serving tray. Pipe a border of buttercream along the edge of the cake and then fill the inside with more buttercream to create an even layer. Sprinkle half of the chopped popping candy and cocoa butter–coated popping candy over the frosting. Use a spatula to spread the popping candy into the frosting. Place the second cake layer on top and repeat the frosting and popping candy and then place the last cake layer on top. Spread an even layer of frosting on the top. Add a thin layer of frosting on the sides of the cake, as a crumb coating so that the cake layers are still visible (to create a naked cake appearance). Or you can frost the sides as well, if you prefer.

Switch from a round tip to a star tip and pipe swirls along the top and/or bottom borders of the cake. Color some of the leftover frosting with pink food coloring, and pipe accent swirls on the cake, if desired. Decorate the cake with the shards of white chocolate popping candy, extra popping candy and gold leaf or glitter on top and on the sides. Refrigerate the cake until ready to serve.

*See photo on page 78.

Juniper Berry Cake with White Chocolate Lime Mousse

I love the flavors of this cake, which remind me of a gin and tonic. The flavor of juniper berries coupled with lime mousse makes this a very refreshing cake. Salted lime might seem like a strange combo to some, but it's one that works really well. Think tequila shots. :)

Makes one 8—inch (20—cm) cake

Juniper Berry Cake

1½ heaping tsp (7 g) juniper berries

115 g (4 oz) unsalted butter

¼ tsp salt

142 g (5 oz) granulated sugar

2 eggs

½ cup (118 ml) milk

1 tsp vanilla extract

115 g (4 oz) all-purpose flour

1 tsp baking powder

Salted White Chocolate Lime Mousse

4 tsp (13 g) powdered gelatin

⅓ cup (79 ml) water

¼ cup (59 ml) whipping cream

455 g (16 oz) white chocolate chips (or chopped white chocolate)

⅔ cup (158 ml) lime juice

½ heaping tsp sea salt

2 cups (473 ml) chilled whipping cream

Juniper Berry Cake

Preheat the oven to 325°F (165°C). Butter and line the bottom of an 8-inch (20-cm) pan with parchment paper and dust the sides with flour.

Heat the juniper berries in a dry pan to toast them, until the berries release their aroma, about 3 minutes. Grind the berries in a spice mill until finely ground.

In a bowl with a hand mixer, cream the butter, salt, juniper berry powder and granulated sugar until fluffy. Add the eggs, one at a time, whisking well after each addition. Whisk in the milk and vanilla. Sift the all-purpose flour and baking powder together, and fold it into the batter in two additions until just mixed through.

Scrape the batter into the prepared pan, and bake for 20 to 25 minutes, until the cake is slightly springy to the touch or a toothpick inserted into the center comes out clean. Remove from the oven and let cool a bit. Turn the cake out onto a cooling rack and let cool completely.

Salted White Chocolate Lime Mousse

Sprinkle the gelatin into a bowl with the water, and mix gently to saturate. Let the gelatin bloom for 5 to 10 minutes.

Combine the bloomed gelatin and ¼ cup (59 ml) cream in a small saucepan and heat over medium heat to melt the gelatin completely. The mixture should be smooth, with no residual gelatin granules (make sure not to let the mixture boil).

Melt the white chocolate in a double boiler over simmering water, stirring frequently, until nice and smooth. Add the gelatin-milk mix, lime juice and salt and whisk well. Mix until the chocolate is smooth with no clumps. Set aside to let the chocolate cool slightly (but not too cold that the gelatin starts to set).

Whisk the 2 cups (473 ml) of whipping cream in a cold bowl (a metal bowl in the freezer for a few minutes usually does the trick), until you have soft peaks. Gently fold the whipped cream into the white chocolate until well incorporated. A few streaks of white chocolate are OK; you don't want to deflate the mousse by overmixing.

Spread the white chocolate mousse over the cake and smooth the top. Refrigerate for at least 4 hours and up to 24 hours.

(continued)

Juniper Berry Cake with White Chocolate Lime Mousse (cont.)

Stabilized Whipped Cream

2 tbsp (30 ml) water

¾ tsp powdered gelatin

1 cup (236 ml) plus ½ tbsp (7 ml) chilled whipping cream, divided

2 tbsp (16 g) confectioners' sugar

To Decorate

Lime slices

Melted white chocolate (optional)

Stabilized Whipped Cream

When ready to assemble, place the water in a small bowl and evenly sprinkle the gelatin over it. Set aside for 10 to 15 minutes to let the gelatin bloom.

Microwave the bloomed gelatin in 10-second intervals, stirring in between, until the gelatin is completely dissolved (take care not to let the gelatin boil).

Add 1 cup (236 ml) of the chilled whipping cream and the confectioners' sugar to a cold bowl. Whisk with the whisk attachment of your hand mixer on medium speed. Add the remaining ½ tablespoon (7 ml) of chilled cream to the hot, dissolved gelatin mix. Add this gradually to the cream that is being whipped (being careful to pour it near the whisk, so that the gelatin gets mixed in with the cream immediately!). Whisk gently until you get stiff peaks. Use immediately.

Decorate

Spread the whipped cream on the top and sides of the cake, over the mousse, or pipe a decorative border. Decorate with lime slices, and drizzle melted white chocolate over the cake, if desired.

Earl Grey Orange Mousse Cake

This cake is a twist on the Jaffa cake flavors, with an Earl Grey vanilla cake and a creamy orange mousse topped with chocolate ganache. It's a light, elegant dessert with floral, fruity flavors.

Makes one 8—inch (20—cm) cake

Earl Grey Cake Layer

½ cup (118 ml) milk

3 bags (or 3 heaped, finely ground tsp [5 g]) Earl Grey tea leaves

115 g (4 oz) unsalted butter

¼ tsp salt

142 g (5 oz) sugar

2 eggs

1 tsp vanilla extract

115 g (4 oz) all-purpose flour

1 tsp baking powder

Orange Mousse

3 tbsp (45 ml) water

1 tsp powdered gelatin

½ cup (118 ml) freshly squeezed orange juice

Zest of 2 oranges

75 g (2.6 oz) sugar

1 cup (236 ml) chilled whipping cream

Chocolate Ganache

170 g (6 oz) semisweet chocolate chips

½ cup (118 ml) whipping cream

Pinch of salt

To Decorate

Orange slices

Earl Grey Cake Layer

Preheat the oven to 325°F (165°C). Butter and line the bottom of an 8-inch (20-cm) pan and dust the sides with flour.

Place the milk and the tea leaves in a small pot and heat until the milk comes to a boil. Then cover the pot and let it simmer over medium-low heat for 2 minutes. Turn off the heat and let the tea infuse the milk until it cools down. Pour the milk mixture into a blender and process to break down the tea leaves. Set aside.

In a bowl using a hand mixer, cream the butter, salt and sugar until fluffy. Add the eggs, one at a time, whisking well after each addition. Whisk in the milk-tea mixture and the vanilla. Sift the all-purpose flour and baking powder together, and fold it into the batter in two additions until just mixed through. Scrape the batter into the prepared pan and bake for 20 to 25 minutes, until the cake is slightly springy to the touch or a toothpick inserted into the center comes out clean. Remove from the oven and let cool slightly. Turn the cake out onto a cooling rack and let cool completely.

Orange Mousse

Place the water in a heatproof bowl and sprinkle the gelatin over it. Let the gelatin bloom for 10 to 15 minutes.

In a saucepan over medium heat, warm the orange juice, orange zest and sugar until the sugar is just melted. Turn off the heat, add the bloomed gelatin and stir to dissolve. Transfer the orange juice to a bowl and let cool to room temperature until slightly thick, but not set.

In another bowl, whip the chilled cream on medium speed until you have soft peaks that hold their shape. Add one-third of the whipped cream to the cooled orange juice and fold it in. Fold in the rest of the whipped cream until just mixed through.

Chocolate Ganache

Place the chocolate in a heatproof bowl, add the cream and salt and melt in 30-second intervals in the microwave, stirring between intervals. When the chocolate has melted, let the ganache cool a little (but still remains pourable).

Decorate

When the cake has cooled and the whipped orange mousse is ready, line the sides of an 8-inch (20-cm) springform with parchment paper or acetate paper and place the cake in the pan. Spread the mousse on top of the cake, and chill for a few hours until the mousse has set.

Once the mousse is set, remove the cake from the springform pan, and gently remove the parchment or acetate paper. Spread the cooled chocolate ganache over the cake, and decorate with orange slices.

Pink Peppercorn
Strawberry and Cream Cheese Cake

This is a decadent twist on the classic strawberry and cream cake. The cake layers are baked with a strawberry cream cheese layer stuffed inside, and the cake is lightly spiced with pink peppercorn, which has a uniquely floral and mild heat that's perfect when paired with strawberry.

Makes one 8–inch (20–cm) cake

Strawberry Layer

455 g (16 oz) fresh strawberries, sliced

2 tbsp (24 g) granulated sugar

Cream Cheese Layer

340 g (12 oz) cream cheese, softened

75 g (2.6 oz) granulated sugar

½ cup (118 ml) strawberry puree

1 drop of red gel food coloring (optional)

1 egg

Pink Peppercorn Vanilla Cake

283 g (10 oz) granulated sugar

2–2½ tsp (6-8 g) whole pink peppercorns, to taste

226 g (8 oz) unsalted butter

¼ tsp salt

4 eggs

⅓ cup (79 ml) milk

2 tsp (10 ml) vanilla extract

226 g (8 oz) all-purpose flour

2 tsp (7 g) baking powder

Strawberry Layer

Place the sliced strawberries in a bowl and add the granulated sugar. Mix well and set aside for 30 to 60 minutes to let the strawberries macerate in the sugar.

Cream Cheese Layer

Place all the ingredients, except the egg, in a bowl. Mix with a hand mixer until smooth and creamy. Add the egg and whisk until just combined.

Pink Peppercorn Vanilla Cake

Preheat the oven to 325°F (165°C). Butter two 8-inch (20-cm) springform pans. Line the bottom with parchment paper and dust the sides with flour.

Place the granulated sugar and peppercorns in a food processor. Process to finely grind the peppercorns.

In a bowl using a hand mixer, cream the butter, salt and peppercorn-sugar mixture until fluffy. Add the eggs, one at a time, whisking well after each addition. Whisk in the milk and vanilla. Sift the all-purpose flour and baking powder together, and fold it into the batter in two additions until just mixed through. Divide two-thirds of the batter between the two prepared pans.

Carefully pour half of the cream cheese layer into the center of each cake, taking care not to let it spread all the way to the edges. This helps the cream cheese layer sink while baking and forms a nice layer in the middle. Dollop half of the remaining cake batter over the cream cheese layer and spread it evenly to cover. Repeat with the rest of the batter on the other cake layer. Gently tap the cake pans on the work surface to remove any air trapped inside the batter.

Bake for 50 to 60 minutes, until the cake surface is slightly springy to the touch or a toothpick inserted into the center comes out clean with only a few cake crumbs attached. Remove from the oven and let cool. Turn the cakes out onto a serving tray and let chill in the fridge overnight, covered.

(continued)

Pink Peppercorn Strawberry and Cream Cheese Cake (cont.)

Stabilized Whipped Cream

¼ cup (59 ml) water

1½ tsp (5 g) powdered gelatin

2 cups (473 ml) plus 1 tbsp (15 ml) chilled whipping cream, divided

2 tsp (10 ml) vanilla extract

½ cup (65 g) confectioners' sugar

To Decorate

Sliced fresh strawberries

Crushed pink peppercorns

Stabilized Whipped Cream

When the cake has cooled, prepare the filling. Place the water in a small bowl and evenly sprinkle the gelatin over it. Set aside for 10 to 15 minutes to let the gelatin bloom. Microwave the bloomed gelatin in 10-second intervals, stirring in between, until the gelatin is completely dissolved (make sure not to let the gelatin boil).

Add 2 cups (473 ml) of the chilled whipping cream and confectioners' sugar to a cold bowl. Whisk with the whisk attachment of your hand mixer on medium speed. Add the remaining 1 tablespoon (15 ml) of chilled cream to the hot, dissolved gelatin mix. Add the gelatin gradually to the cream that is being whipped (being careful to pour it near the whisk, so that the gelatin gets mixed in with the cream immediately!). Add the vanilla and confectioners' sugar. Whisk gently until you get stiff peaks. Use immediately.

Decorate

Place one cake layer on a serving tray. Then place half of the whipped cream on top and top this with half of the macerated strawberries. Top with the second cake layer and then whipped cream and strawberries. Decorate with extra strawberries and pink peppercorn.

Keep the cake refrigerated until ready to serve.

Pavlova Summer Cheesecake

This cake is a nod to my Kiwi and Australian background. I love a good pavlova with fresh summery fruits, but this pavlova cheesecake might be my new favorite. It's a crispy, marshmallowy pavlova topped with a fruity, tangy cheesecake and all the classic pavlova toppings. It's sure to brighten up any summer party!

Makes one 8—inch (20—cm) cake

Pavlova

200 g (7 oz) granulated sugar

1 tbsp (6 g) cornflour (cornstarch)

4 egg whites

Pinch of cream of tartar

Pinch of salt

2 tsp (10 ml) vanilla extract

1 tsp white vinegar

Raspberry Cheesecake Layer

¼ cup (59 ml) water

2 tsp (6 g) powdered gelatin

170 g (6 oz) frozen raspberries, thawed and pureed (pureed fresh raspberries are fine, too)

455 g (16 oz) cream cheese, softened

100 g (3.5 oz) granulated sugar

1 cup (236 ml) chilled whipping cream

Pavlova

Preheat the oven to 250°F (120°C). Line a baking sheet with parchment paper and draw one 7-inch (18-cm) circle on it. Turn the parchment paper over, so that the drawn circle is facing the bottom but you can still see the lines through the paper.

In a dry food processor, process the granulated sugar until you have superfine sugar granules. Add the cornflour and mix to combine.

Place the egg whites in a clean, dry metal bowl of your stand mixer (you can use a hand mixer or a stand mixer for this, but it'll be easier in a stand mixer). Add the cream of tartar and salt. Whisk on high speed until you have soft peaks. Lower the speed to medium, and gradually add the superfine sugar while continuously whisking the egg whites. Once all the sugar has been added, scrape down the sides of the bowl to get any sugar that may have stuck to the sides. Whisk the egg whites on medium-high speed for another 5 to 7 minutes, until all the sugar crystals have completely dissolved. (You can check if the sugar has dissolved by rubbing some of the egg whites between your fingers every couple of minutes—if the sugar has dissolved, the egg whites will feel smooth; if it feels gritty, the meringue is not ready yet.) As soon as the sugar has dissolved, add the vanilla and vinegar and whisk on high speed for a minute to combine.

Dollop the batter in the drawn circle and spread it to fill the circle evenly. Using a flat spatula, make sure the edges are as straight as possible. Bake for 1 hour. Turn off the oven and let the pavlova cool completely inside the oven, with the oven door left ajar. (The pavlova shouldn't crack or collapse too much if it hasn't been over beaten. But even if there's some cracking on the surface, don't sweat it: you'll be topping it up with the cheesecake layer.)

Raspberry Cheesecake Layer

Place the water in a heatproof bowl. Sprinkle the gelatin over the surface of the water and let the gelatin bloom for 10 to 15 minutes.

Place the pureed raspberries in a saucepan with the bloomed gelatin. Heat over medium heat just until the gelatin melts. Set the raspberry puree aside to cool.

Mix the cream cheese and granulated sugar in a bowl until creamy and smooth. Add the cooled raspberries and mix to combine.

In a separate bowl, whisk the cream on medium speed until you have soft peaks. Fold the whipped cream into the cream cheese mixture just to combine.

(continued)

Pavlova Summer Cheesecake (cont.)

Whipped Cream Topping

1 cup (236 ml) chilled whipping cream

¼ cup (33 g) confectioners' sugar

To Decorate

Raspberries

Sliced strawberries

Sliced kiwi

Sliced mango

Passion fruit pulp

Whipped Cream Topping

When ready to serve, add the chilled whipping cream and confectioners' sugar to a cold bowl. Gently whisk with the whisk attachment of your hand mixer on medium speed until you get soft peaks. Use immediately.

Assembly

Line the bottom of an 8-inch (20-cm) springform pan with parchment paper, and the sides with parchment paper or acetate paper. Place the pavlova at the bottom of the pan (if the pavlova doesn't fit, you can create an acetate paper sleeve to fit around the pavlova instead). Top the pavlova with the raspberry cheesecake layer and spread it evenly. Refrigerate for a few hours to let it set.

Decorate

Carefully unmold the cake and remove the parchment paper. Spread the whipped cream over the cake, decorate with the sliced fruits and drizzle with the passion fruit pulp. The pavlova should be served the day of assembly, so that it doesn't become soggy. Serve immediately.

Chocolate-Covered Strawberry Mousse Cake

Another classic combo, this strawberry mousse layer is made with thick strawberry pie filling.
A great dessert to serve on Valentine's Day!

Makes one 8—inch (2Ø—cm) cake

Fudgy Brownie Layer

115 g (4 oz) bittersweet chocolate, chopped

115 g (4 oz) unsalted butter

142 g (5 oz) sugar

¼ tsp salt

1 tsp vanilla extract

2 eggs

94 g (3.3 oz) all-purpose flour

Strawberry Mousse

6 tbsp (89 ml) water, divided

1½ tsp (5.3 g) powdered gelatin

455 g (16 oz) strawberries, hulled (fresh or frozen)

150 g (5.3 oz) sugar

2 tbsp (6 g) cornflour

226 g (8 oz) cream cheese, softened

1 cup (236 ml) chilled whipping cream

Chocolate Ganache

340 g (12 oz) semisweet chocolate chips

1 cup (236 ml) whipping cream

Pinch of salt

Fresh strawberries, blotted dry, for garnish

Fudgy Brownie Layer

Preheat the oven to 350°F (180°C). Butter an 8-inch (20-cm) wide, 3-inch (8-cm) tall springform pan. Line the bottom with parchment paper and dust the sides with flour.

Melt the chocolate and butter in a heatproof bowl in the microwave in 30-second intervals, stirring in between to prevent the chocolate from burning. Let the chocolate-butter mixture cool. Add the sugar, salt and vanilla, and whisk to combine. Next, add the eggs, one at a time, whisking after each addition. Fold in the flour until just combined. Pour the batter into the prepared cake pan and bake for 20 to 25 minutes. Remove from the oven and let cool for a few hours. Loosen the brownie layer from the springform pan, and refrigerate until needed.

Strawberry Mousse

Place 3 tablespoons of the water in a small bowl and evenly sprinkle the gelatin over it. Set aside for 10 to 15 minutes to let the gelatin bloom.

Place the strawberries and sugar in a saucepan. Heat over medium heat, stirring frequently to melt the sugar. Bring the mixture to a boil and let it simmer for 20 minutes (less, if using fresh strawberries), until the strawberries have softened and the liquid is syrupy. Dissolve the cornflour in the remaining 3 tablespoons (44 ml) water. Add this to the strawberry syrup and let it cook for a few more minutes until thickened. Remove the saucepan from the heat and add the bloomed gelatin. Whisk to completely dissolve the gelatin in the residual heat. Let the strawberry topping cool in a bowl until needed. Add the cream cheese and chilled whipping cream to a cold bowl. Whisk with the whisk attachment on your hand mixer on medium speed until smooth and fluffy. Fold in the cooled strawberry mixture until well combined. Spread it evenly over the cooled brownie layer. Refrigerate until set.

Chocolate Ganache

Place the semisweet chocolate in a heatproof bowl. Add the cream and salt and microwave in 30-second intervals, stirring in between, until the chocolate has melted. Stir to make sure the ganache is smooth and let cool to a thick but pourable consistency. Once the strawberry layer has set, cover the cake with most of the chocolate ganache. Before the chocolate layer sets, dip the fresh strawberries in the remaining ganache, and place them on top of the cake. Refrigerate the cake until ready to serve.

Chocolate Peanut Dacquoise Cake

This is a Snickers candy bar in cake form. The salted caramel and nougat come together to make the buttercream, and the peanuts are studded in a crispy, chewy layer of meringue tucked away in the middle. Yes, there are many parts to this secret-layer cake, but they all come together beautifully.

Makes one 8–inch (20–cm) cake

Chocolate Cake Layer

400 g (14 oz) unsalted butter

½ tsp salt

450 g (15.8 oz) granulated sugar

250 g (8.8 oz) all-purpose flour

1 tsp baking soda

¾ cup (177 ml) strongly brewed coffee, hot

85 g (3 oz) cocoa powder, sifted

2 tsp (10 ml) vanilla extract

115 g (4 oz) bittersweet chocolate, melted

170 g (6 oz) sour cream

4 eggs

Peanut Dacquoise

200 g (7 oz) granulated sugar

170 g (6 oz) roasted salted peanuts

1 tbsp (9 g) cornflour

4 large egg whites

Pinch of cream of tartar

Pinch of salt

1 tsp vanilla extract

Salted Caramel Sauce

200 g (7 oz) granulated sugar

¼ cup (59 ml) water

Chocolate Cake Layer

Preheat the oven to 325°F (160°C). Butter and line the bottom of two 8-inch (20-cm) pans with parchment paper and dust the sides with cocoa powder.

In a bowl using a hand mixer, cream the butter, salt and granulated sugar until light and fluffy. Sift the all-purpose flour and baking soda together into a bowl.

In a separate bowl, combine the hot coffee, cocoa powder, vanilla and melted chocolate, and whisk until blended. Add the sour cream and stir to combine. Add the eggs, one at a time, to the creamed butter and sugar, mixing well after each addition. Add half of the chocolate mixture and whisk until well combined. Fold in half of the flour to combine. Repeat with the remaining half of the chocolate mixture and finish with the remaining half of the flour mixture. Divide the cake batter between the prepared pans and spread it evenly. Tap the cake pans on the counter a couple of times to remove any gas bubbles trapped inside. Bake for 40–60 minutes, until a toothpick inserted into the center comes out clean. Remove the cakes from the oven and let cool.

Peanut Dacquoise

Preheat the oven to 250°F (120°C). Line a baking sheet with parchment paper and draw two 7-inch (18-cm) circles on it. Turn the parchment paper over, so that the drawn circles are facing the bottom but you can still see the lines through the paper.

In a dry food processor, process the granulated sugar until you have superfine sugar granules. Transfer the sugar to a dry bowl. Place the roasted salted peanuts and cornflour in the food processor. Process until the peanuts are finely ground.

Place the egg whites in a clean, dry metal bowl of your stand mixer. Add the cream of tartar and salt. Whisk on high speed until you have soft peaks. Lower the speed to medium, and gradually add the sugar while continuously whisking the egg whites. Once all the sugar has been added, scrape down the sides of the bowl to get any sugar that may have stuck to the sides. Whisk the egg whites on medium-high speed for another 5 to 7 minutes, until all the sugar crystals have completely dissolved. Stir in the vanilla. Fold in the ground peanuts in two additions, being careful not to deflate the egg mixture. Divide the mixture equally between the two circles and spread it evenly inside the drawn lines. Bake for 2 hours. Turn off the oven and let the dacquoise cool completely in the oven, about 2 hours. Set aside one layer for assembling the cake. Crush the other layer; this will be used to decorate the cake.

(continued)

Chocolate Peanut
Dacquoise Cake (cont.)

2 tbsp (30 ml) corn syrup

½ cup (118 ml) whipping cream, warmed

1 tsp coarse salt

2 tsp (10 ml) vanilla extract

Peanut Butter Nougat

115 g (4 oz) unsalted butter

100 g (3.5 oz) granulated sugar

¼ cup (61 g) evaporated milk

¼ cup (45 g) smooth peanut butter

1½ cups (339 g) marshmallow crème

Salted Caramel Peanut Butter Nougat Frosting

226 g (8 oz) unsalted butter

115 g (4 oz) confectioners' sugar

1-2 tbsp (15–30 ml) whipping cream

Fudgy Chocolate Frosting

340 g (12 oz) unsalted butter, softened

½ tsp salt

115 g (4 oz) confectioners' sugar

2 tbsp (14 g) good-quality natural cocoa

340 g (12 oz) semisweet chocolate, melted and cooled

2 tsp (10 ml) vanilla extract

Up to ¼ cup (60 ml) whipping cream

Salted Caramel Sauce

Add the granulated sugar, water and corn syrup to a saucepan over medium heat and swirl to combine. Let the sugar dissolve without stirring the liquid, as this could crystallize the sugar. Let the sugar syrup come to a boil and gradually change color to dark golden amber. Add the warm cream to the sugar, slowly, while whisking. Add the salt and vanilla. Whisk to combine the cream with the sugar until you get a smooth caramel sauce, 2 to 5 minutes. Let it cool, pour into a glass jar and set aside until needed.

Peanut Butter Nougat

Combine the butter, granulated sugar and evaporated milk in a saucepan over low heat, stirring occasionally until the sugar dissolves and the mixture comes to a boil. Boil for 1 to 2 minutes. Remove from the heat and stir to make sure it's smooth. Add the peanut butter and marshmallow crème, and whisk until well incorporated. Let cool to room temperature.

Salted Caramel Peanut Butter Nougat Frosting

Place the peanut butter nougat and ¼ cup (57 g) of salted caramel sauce in a bowl and whisk to combine. Add the butter and confectioners' sugar and whisk until light and fluffy. Add 1 to 2 tablespoons (15 to 30 ml) of cream to make the frosting more creamy if needed. The frosting will be soft, so make sure it is at room temperate or slightly chilled to make it easier to use.

Fudgy Chocolate Frosting

In a bowl using a mixer with the whisk attachment, whisk the butter and salt until light and fluffy. Add the confectioners' sugar and cocoa powder, a little at a time, mixing on low speed (to prevent a sugar storm!). Once all the confectioners' sugar is mixed in, increase the speed to medium-high and whisk until creamy, light and fluffy. Add the melted and cooled chocolate in a stream and whisk until the frosting is light and fluffy and the chocolate is mixed through. Whisk in the vanilla. Add the cream, 1 tablespoon (15 ml) at a time, until you have a creamy, light buttercream, at the desired consistency (I added all the cream so that I had a very light and creamy buttercream).

Decorate

Place one cake layer on a serving tray. Spread half of the salted caramel peanut butter nougat frosting on top of the cake. Drizzle some salted caramel sauce over the frosting. Next, place one peanut butter dacquoise on top. Then spread the other half of the salted caramel peanut butter nougat frosting and drizzle with more salted caramel sauce. Top with the second layer of chocolate cake. Frost the cake with the fudgy chocolate frosting and decorate with frosting swirls. Drizzle more salted caramel sauce over the cake. Refrigerate the cake until ready to serve. Place the crushed peanut dacquoise pieces on top just before serving. This cake is best served at room temperature.

Cheesecake-Stuffed Devil's Food Cake

This is the kind of chocolate cake that'll stop people in their tracks. A super fudgy, dense chocolate cake with cream cheese in the middle—this devil's food cake is a force to be reckoned with! This makes an amazing birthday cake.

Makes one 8—inch (20—cm) cake

Cheesecake Filling

455 g (16 oz) cream cheese, softened

100 g (3.5 oz) granulated sugar

1 tsp vanilla extract

½ cup (118 ml) whipping cream

2 eggs

Fudgy Devil's Food Cake

400 g (14 oz) unsalted butter

½ tsp salt

450 g (15.8 oz) granulated sugar

250 g (8.8 oz) all-purpose flour

1 tsp baking soda

¾ cup (177 ml) strongly brewed coffee, hot

85 g (3 oz) cocoa powder, sifted

2 tsp vanilla extract

115 g (4 oz) bittersweet chocolate, melted

170 g (6 oz) sour cream

4 eggs

Cheesecake Filling

Place all the ingredients, except the eggs, in a bowl. Mix on medium speed until smooth and creamy. Add the eggs and mix until just combined. Cover and set aside until you have the chocolate cake batter ready.

Fudgy Devil's Food Cake

Preheat the oven to 325°F (160°C). Butter and line the bottom of two 8-inch (20-cm) pans with parchment paper and dust the sides with cocoa powder.

In the bowl of a mixer, cream the butter, salt and granulated sugar until light and fluffy.

Sift the all-purpose flour and baking soda together into a bowl.

In a separate bowl, combine the hot coffee, cocoa powder, vanilla and melted chocolate, and whisk until smooth. Add the sour cream and stir to combine.

Add the eggs, one at a time, to the creamed butter and sugar, mixing well after each addition. Add half of the chocolate mixture and mix until well combined (I like to mix by hand, but you can use the low speed on your mixer for this). Fold in half of the flour mixture to combine (or use the low speed on your mixer). Repeat with the remaining half of the chocolate mixture and finish with the remaining half of the flour mixture.

Divide two-thirds of the cake batter between the two cake pans. Next, pour half of the cheesecake filling into the middle of each cake (take care not to let the cheesecake spread all the way to the edges). Divide the remaining chocolate batter between the two cake layers to cover the cheesecake filling as evenly as possible. Tap the cake pans on the counter a couple of times to remove any gas bubbles trapped inside.

Bake for 50 to 60 minutes, until a toothpick inserted into the center comes out clean. Remove the cakes from the oven and let cool (the cakes will sink slightly in the middle, and that is OK). Release the cakes from the pans.

(continued)

Cheesecake-Stuffed
Devil's Food Cake (cont.)

Fudgy Chocolate Frosting

340 g (12 oz) unsalted butter, softened

½ tsp salt

115 g (4 oz) confectioners' sugar

2 tbsp (14 g) good-quality natural cocoa

340 g (12 oz) semisweet chocolate, melted and cooled

2 tsp vanilla extract

Up to ¼ cup (59 ml) whipping cream

To Decorate

Sifted confectioners' sugar

Fudgy Chocolate Frosting

In a bowl using a mixer with the whisk attachment, whisk the butter and salt until light and fluffy. Add the confectioners' sugar and cocoa powder, a little at a time, mixing on low speed (to prevent a sugar storm!). Once all the confectioners' sugar is mixed in, increase the speed to medium-high and whisk until creamy, light and fluffy.

Add the melted and cooled chocolate in a stream and whisk until the frosting is light and fluffy and the chocolate has mixed through. Whisk in the vanilla. Add the cream, 1 tablespoon (15 ml) at a time, until you have a creamy, light buttercream, at the desired consistency (I added all the cream so that I had a very light and creamy buttercream).

Decorate

Place one cake layer on a serving tray. Then place a generous amount of fudgy chocolate frosting on top and spread it to create an even layer (since the cake will be slightly sunken in in the middle, there will be more frosting in the middle than at the edges). Top with the second cake layer. Frost the sides of the cake with the fudgy chocolate frosting. You can create rough swirls for a rustic look, or smooth the sides for a straight edge. Place the remaining frosting in a pastry bag with an open star tip. Pipe decorative swirls at the top. Dust the cake with confectioners' sugar and serve.

Nutella and Berry
Queen of Puddings

Queen of puddings is a classic British bread pudding. I grew up eating this dessert a lot, and decided to kick it up a notch with a chocolatey Nutella filling. Everyone likes Nutella-stuffed French toast, so I figured, why not bread pudding with a Nutella filling, topped with berry preserves and a marshmallowy meringue?

Makes one 8–inch (20–cm) cake

Bread Pudding

1 cup (236 ml) milk

1 cup (236 ml) cream (or substitute 1 cup [236 ml] milk and 1 cup [236 ml] cream with 2 cups [473 ml] half-and-half)

100 g (3.5 oz) sugar

2 tsp (10 ml) vanilla extract

2 eggs

340 g (12 oz) stale brioche or challah bread, cut into 1-inch (2.5-cm) cubes

225 g (8 oz) Nutella (or any hazelnut spread)

Berry Layer

1½ cups (333 g) berry preserves

1 cup (166 g) sliced strawberries

Meringue Layer

3 egg whites

100 g (3.5 oz) sugar

Pinch of salt

Pinch of cream of tartar

1 tsp vanilla extract

Bread Pudding

Preheat the oven to 350°F (180°C). Butter an 8-inch (20-cm) wide, 3-inch (8-cm) tall springform pan, line the bottom with parchment paper and dust the sides with flour.

Whisk the milk, cream, sugar, vanilla and eggs in a bowl. Gently press the bread cubes into the mixture and let them get saturated for a few minutes.

Place two-thirds of the soaked bread and egg mixture in the prepared pan. Gently press it down to create an even layer. Dollop the Nutella over the surface and spread it out as evenly as you can (do not spread all the way to the edges). Top the Nutella layer with the remaining bread and egg mixture, and spread it to completely cover the Nutella layer.

Bake for 20 to 30 minutes, until the custard is set but slightly soft in the middle. Remove from the oven.

Berry Layer

While the bread pudding is still hot, spread berry preserves on top and layer with the sliced strawberries.

Meringue Layer

Bring some water to a boil in a saucepan. Then lower the heat to bring it to a simmer.

Combine the egg whites, sugar, salt and cream of tartar in a clean, dry metal bowl. Place the metal bowl over the simmering water (be careful not to let the water mix with your egg whites), and whisk continuously to dissolve the sugar, 5 to 10 minutes. (You can check if the sugar has dissolved by rubbing some of the egg whites between your fingers—if the sugar has dissolved, the egg whites will be smooth; if it feels gritty, it's not there yet.)

When the sugar is completely dissolved, remove the egg whites from the double boiler and whisk on high speed using a whisk attachment on a hand mixer or stand mixer until doubled in volume, the egg whites are thick and glossy and the bowl is cool to the touch. Add the vanilla and whisk for 1 minute. Use immediately.

Decorate

If you are serving the bread pudding warm, top it with the meringue while it is still warm and use a blowtorch to caramelize the meringue. Alternatively, you can serve the bread pudding cold or at room temperature. Let the bread pudding (with the berry preserves on top) cool to room temperature and then cover and refrigerate until needed. Top with the meringue and caramelize the surface with a blowtorch or under a broiler just before serving.

No-Bake Cakes

No-bake desserts let you think outside the box, be creative and come up with easy and fun desserts that you can put together in no time at all. While you can incorporate an array of secret ingredients and layers in no-bake cakes, my favorite is popping candy! There's something just so fundamentally exciting about the fizzy candy popping inside your mouth that appeals to the inner kid in me. But I also love mixing and matching flavors and textures for that hidden wow factor—like with the Panettone Trifle Cake (page 154) or the Mexican Hot Chocolate Cookie Pudding (page 148)!

No-Bake
Popping Raspberry
Chocolate Truffle Cake

If the decadent chocolate layer packed with the flavor of raspberries doesn't get you, then it'll be the crust that pops and fizzles in your mouth as you eat it. This is an indulgent dessert, so it'll serve quite a few, but that only means there's more love to be shared around!

Makes one 8-inch (20-cm) cake

Popping Candy Crust

200 g (7 oz) Biscoff cookies

2 tbsp (28 g) brown sugar

56 g (2 oz) unsalted butter, melted

35 g (1 oz) popping candy (cocoa butter coated or strawberry flavored is OK too)

Raspberry Chocolate Truffle

455 g (16 oz) semisweet chocolate

¾ cup (177 ml) whipping cream, divided

115 g (4 oz) raspberries (fresh or frozen)

Pinch of salt

Popping Candy Crust

Line the bottom of an 8-inch (20-cm) pastry ring or a springform pan with parchment paper. Line the sides with acetate paper or parchment paper (so that it's easier to remove at the end).

Process the Biscoff cookies in a food processor to form crumbs. Add the brown sugar and butter, while processing (the crumbs should stick together). Transfer the cookie crumbs to a bowl, add the popping candy and mix in gently.

Press the crumbs into the bottom of the prepared pan (you don't have to press too hard, just firm enough to form a flat surface). Put the crust in the freezer to set.

Raspberry Chocolate Truffle

Place the semisweet chocolate, ½ cup (118 ml) of the cream, raspberries and salt in a heatproof bowl. Microwave in 45-second intervals, stirring in between, until the chocolate has melted. The raspberries will break up and mix in with the chocolate. Let the chocolate mixture cool. When it's cool to the touch and has thickened, whip the remaining ¼ cup (59 ml) of cream to stiff peaks and fold it into the chocolate. Pour this over the frozen cookie crust. Place the cake in the freezer for at least a few hours until frozen.

(continued)

No-Bake *Popping Raspberry* Chocolate Truffle Cake (cont.)

Chocolate Fudge Glaze

⅓ cup (79 ml) water

3 tsp (9 g) powdered gelatin

⅔ cup (158 ml) whipping cream

3 tbsp (44 ml) corn syrup

50 g (1.7 oz) granulated sugar

70 g (2.5 oz) brown sugar

30 g (1 oz) cocoa powder

¼ tsp kosher salt

200 g (7 oz) semisweet chocolate, chopped or chips

2 tbsp (29 g) unsalted butter

To Decorate

Freeze-dried raspberry powder

2 tbsp (12 g) popping candy

Pink luster dust

Fresh raspberries

Chocolate Fudge Glaze

Place the water in a small bowl and sprinkle the gelatin over the surface. Let the gelatin soak up the water and bloom for 10 to 15 minutes.

Place the whipping cream, corn syrup, granulated sugar, brown sugar, cocoa powder and salt in a saucepan over medium-high heat. Whisk to melt the sugars and cocoa powder and bring to a boil. Reduce the heat to medium and let it simmer for about 5 minutes.

Remove the pan from the heat and stir in the chopped chocolate and butter. Finally, add the bloomed gelatin and stir to dissolve. Let cool (but not set).

Decorate

Remove the frozen truffle cake from the freezer. Then gently remove it from the pan, and place it on top of a tall but stable glass (or cylindrical object that can support the cake—this is to catch runoff fudge sauce that we are going to pour over it next). Pour the cooled chocolate fudge sauce over the cake, making sure it completely coats the top and the sides. Use a spatula to spread the sauce. Let the chocolate glaze set. Keep the truffle cake in the fridge to let it soften (until you're ready to serve).

Mix the freeze-dried raspberry powder and popping candy in a bowl. Sprinkle the popping candy over the surface of the cake, and decorate with luster dust and fresh raspberries just before serving. When ready to serve, slice the cake with a warm knife to get clean edges.

Wake-Me-Up
Breakfast Cheesecake

If you're a dessert-for-breakfast kind of person, then this cheesecake has your name written all over it! The cheesecake is made with cornflakes-infused cream (cereal milk) atop a Fruity Pebbles crust with a fizzy, exploding, popping candy hidden inside.

Makes one 8-inch (20-cm) cake

Fruity Pebbles Crust

142 g (5 oz) Fruity Pebbles cereal

4-6 tbsp (57-86 g) unsalted butter, melted

20 g (0.7 oz) popping candy

200 g (7 oz) white chocolate, melted

Cornflakes-Infused Cream

4 cups (112 g) cornflakes cereal

4 cups (946 ml) whipping cream

No-Bake Cornflakes Cheesecake

3 tbsp (44 ml) water

1½ tsp (5 g) powdered gelatin

455 g (16 oz) cream cheese, softened

½ cup (65 g) confectioners' sugar

1 tsp vanilla extract

Fruity Pebbles Crust

Line the bottom of an 8-inch (20-cm) springform pan with parchment paper and the sides with parchment paper or acetate paper. Alternatively, you can simply use a pie dish.

Process the Fruity Pebbles cereal in a food processor until you get coarse crumbs. Add as much of the melted butter as needed to make the crumbs sticky enough to form a crust. Press the crushed cereal into the prepared pan to form a firm crust. Freeze the crust.

Stir the popping candy into the melted (and slightly cooled) white chocolate. Once the crust is frozen (1 to 2 hours), dollop and spread the mixture on top of the crust, taking care not to crush the popping candy. Keep frozen until needed.

Cornflakes-Infused Cream

To toast cornflakes in the oven: Preheat the oven to 300°F (150°C). Spread the cornflakes on a baking sheet and bake for 10 to 15 minutes, until lightly toasted. The cornflakes should be slightly darker, but not burned.

To toast cornflakes on the stove: Heat a large nonstick pan over medium-high heat. Toast the cornflakes in the hot pan, stirring and shaking frequently, until they become a shade darker, being careful not to burn them.

Place the cream in a jug or a bowl and add the hot cornflakes from the oven or stove. Let the cornflakes infuse the cream for 30 minutes. Strain the cream through a fine sieve or a nut milk bag. Squeeze out as much of the liquid as possible. Cover and return the cream to the fridge to let it chill. You should get 2½ to 3 cups (592 to 710 ml) of infused cream.

No-Bake Cornflakes Cheesecake

Place the water in a heatproof bowl. Sprinkle the gelatin evenly over the water and let the gelatin bloom for 10 to 15 minutes. Microwave the bloomed gelatin in 10-second intervals, stirring in between, until the gelatin is completely dissolved (taking care not to let the gelatin boil).

In a bowl with a mixer, combine the cream cheese, confectioners' sugar and vanilla until smooth. Add 1 cup (236 ml) of cornflakes-infused cream, and whisk again until the mixture is fluffy and creamy. Add the gelatin gradually while whisking. Scrape the cream cheese mixture on top of the frozen crust and smooth the top. Place the cheesecake in the fridge and let it set for a few hours. Keep it refrigerated until you're ready to serve.

(continued)

Wake-Me-Up
Breakfast Cheesecake (cont.)

Stabilized Cornflakes–Infused Whipped Cream

2 tbsp (30 ml) water

¾ tsp (2 g) powdered gelatin

¼ cup (33 g) confectioners' sugar

2 tsp (10 ml) vanilla extract or vanilla bean paste

To Decorate

½ cup (14 g) cornflakes, crushed

Extra Fruity Pebbles cereal, crushed

Stabilized Cornflakes–Infused Whipped Cream

Place the water in a heatproof bowl and evenly sprinkle the gelatin over it. Set aside for 10 to 15 minutes to let the gelatin bloom. Microwave the bloomed gelatin in 10-second intervals, stirring in between, until the gelatin is completely dissolved (taking care not to let the gelatin boil).

Add 1 cup (236 ml) of the chilled infused whipping cream, confectioners' sugar and vanilla in a cold bowl. Whisk with the whisk attachment of your hand mixer on medium speed. Add ½ tablespoon (7 ml) of chilled infused cream to the hot, dissolved gelatin mix. Add this gradually to the cream that is being whipped (being careful to pour it near the whisk, so that the gelatin gets mixed in with the cream immediately!). Whisk gently until you get stiff peaks. Transfer the cream to a pastry bag with a pastry tip. Use immediately.

Decorate

Pipe the whipped cream on top of the cheesecake layer. Sprinkle with the crushed cornflakes and Fruity Pebbles cereal before serving.

No-Bake *Cherry Ripe* Cheesecake

Cherry Ripe is a popular candy bar in Australia and New Zealand. Think Almond Joy or Bounty, but with cherries—a coconut cherry bar dipped in dark chocolate. This cake is made with fresh black cherries, giving the filling a purple color, but you can use any sweet cherry. The fudgy, nutty cherry filling sits on an Oreo crust and is topped with a dark chocolate cheesecake layer. It's a cherry pie, cheesecake and candy bar all in one.

Makes one 8-inch (20-cm) cake

Oreo Crust

283 g (10 oz) regular Oreos

6 tbsp (86 g) unsalted butter, melted

Pinch of salt

Cherry Ripe Filling

170 g (6 oz) black cherries (fresh or thawed from frozen)

200 g (7 oz) desiccated coconut

200 g (7 oz) sweetened condensed milk

2 tbsp (30 ml) coconut milk

Chocolate Cheesecake Topping

455 g (16 oz) cream cheese, softened

115 g (4 oz) confectioners' sugar

¼ cup (30 g) sour cream

170 g (6 oz) semisweet chocolate, melted

Chocolate Ganache

340 g (12 oz) semisweet chocolate chips

1 cup (236 ml) whipping cream

Pinch of salt

To Decorate

Fresh cherries

Shaved coconut

Oreo Crust

Line the bottom of an 8-inch (20-cm) springform pan with parchment paper and the sides with parchment paper or acetate paper.

Place the Oreos in a food processor, and process until you have crumbs. Add the melted butter and salt and pulse to combine. Press the crumbs into the bottom of the prepared pan and press a roughly 1-inch (2.5-cm) tall wall around the edges to create a crust. Freeze the crust.

Cherry Ripe Filling

Place the cherries in a food processor and pulse to chop. Combine the chopped cherries, desiccated coconut, sweetened condensed milk and coconut milk in a saucepan over medium heat and heat until the coconut absorbs the liquid and is simmering (about 10 minutes, depending on the heat). Let the cherry filling cool.

Pour the cooled cherry filling into the pan with the Oreo crust to fill the crust. Then keep it in the fridge to set.

Chocolate Cheesecake Topping

Mix the cream cheese, confectioners' sugar and sour cream in a bowl until smooth and creamy. Add the melted chocolate and mix to combine. Top the cherry filling with the chocolate cheesecake topping and let it set in the fridge.

Chocolate Ganache

Place the semisweet chocolate in a heatproof bowl. Add the cream and salt and microwave in 30-second intervals, stirring in between, until the chocolate has melted. Stir to make sure the ganache is smooth and let cool to a thick but pourable consistency.

Decorate

When the cheesecake has set, release the cake from the springform pan and pour the ganache over the top. Either spread the ganache on top of the cake or coat the entire cake. Decorate with fresh cherries and shaved coconut on top.

Mexican Hot Chocolate Cookie Pudding

This gorgeous layered, no-bake dessert is inspired by a Sri Lankan classic—chocolate cookie (biscuit) pudding. Instead of using only regular chocolate, I combined it with Mexican chocolate and then topped it all with marshmallows. There's cinnamon and spices in the pudding, and cream and marshmallows on top. It's like a decadent hot chocolate, but better!

Makes one 8-inch (20-cm) cake

Mexican Chocolate French Buttercream

6 egg yolks

3 eggs

½ tsp ground cinnamon

½ tsp cayenne pepper

300 g (10.5 oz) granulated sugar

½ tsp kosher salt

455 g (16 oz) unsalted butter, softened

142 g (5 oz) bittersweet chocolate, melted

142 g (5 oz) plain Mexican chocolate, melted

2 tsp vanilla extract

Stabilized Whipped Cream

3 tbsp (44 ml) water

1½ tsp (5 g) powdered gelatin

2 cups (473 ml) plus 1 tbsp (15 ml) chilled whipping cream, divided

½ cup (65 g) confectioners' sugar

1 tsp vanilla extract

Mexican Chocolate French Buttercream

Place the egg yolks, eggs, cinnamon, cayenne pepper and granulated sugar in a metal bowl. Using a mixer, whisk until pale and frothy.

Bring some water to a boil in a saucepan. Lower the heat to a simmer. Place the metal bowl over the simmering water and whisk continuously until the sugar has completely melted.

If you'd like to pasteurize the eggs, bring the temperature of the egg-sugar mixture to 150°F (66°C) and retain the heat at this temperature for 10 minutes (remember to continuously whisk the egg yolks so that they don't cook and harden!).

Remove the bowl from the simmering water. Add the salt and whisk on medium speed until the bowl is cool to the touch (this is important—or it'll be too hot for the butter, and will result in a runny frosting). Add the softened butter 1 to 2 tablespoons (15 to 30 ml) at a time, whisking well between each addition. The frosting will appear runny and broken, but keep adding all of the butter and it'll become smooth and creamy.

Melt the bittersweet and Mexican chocolates in the microwave or over a double boiler. Let cool. Add the cooled, melted chocolate and vanilla and whisk to combine. Keep the frosting covered until needed. Mix with a spatula to make it smooth just before using.

Stabilized Whipped Cream

When ready to assemble the cake, place the water in a small heatproof bowl and evenly sprinkle the gelatin over it. Set aside for 10 to 15 minutes to let the gelatin bloom. Microwave the bloomed gelatin in 10-second intervals, stirring in between, until the gelatin is completely dissolved (it's important that you don't let the gelatin boil).

Add 2 cups (473 ml) of the chilled whipping cream, confectioners' sugar and vanilla to a cold bowl. Whisk with the whisk attachment of your hand mixer on medium speed. Add the remaining 1 tablespoon (15 ml) of chilled cream to the hot, dissolved gelatin mix. Add this gradually to the cream that is being whipped (being careful to pour it near the whisk, so that the gelatin gets mixed in with the cream immediately!). Whisk on medium speed until you get soft peaks, and use it immediately.

(continued)

Mexican Hot Chocolate Cookie Pudding (cont.)

Cookie Layer

285–425 g (10–15 oz) Maria cookies

1 cup (236 ml) milk, warmed

To Decorate

Marshmallows

Extra grated Mexican chocolate

Cookie Layer

Line an 8-inch (20-cm) springform pan on the bottom with parchment paper, and line the sides with acetate paper or parchment paper.

Soak the cookies, about two at a time, in the warm milk for a second or two and place them on the bottom of the pan, letting them overlap. Then spread a layer of Mexican chocolate French buttercream over it. Repeat with milk-soaked cookies and buttercream for at least four or five cookie layers, ending with a buttercream layer. Top the buttercream with the stabilized whipped cream. Refrigerate for at least a few hours (or even overnight).

Decorate

Carefully remove the cake from the pan. Line the edge of the cake with marshmallows and toast them using a blowtorch. Sprinkle with grated chocolate. This is best eaten as soon as the marshmallows have been toasted and the buttercream is slightly softened.

Black Forest Mousse Cake

This dessert was inspired by the classic Black Forest cake. This rendition features light and airy dark chocolate and white chocolate mousse layers, topped with whipped cream and chocolate shavings. The secret, though, is that juicy and boozy cherry filling hiding between the two chocolate layers. Plus, this mousse cake is deceptively easy to make.

Makes one 8-inch (20-cm) cake

Cherry Filling

¼ cup (59 ml) water

1½ tsp (5 g) powdered gelatin

340 g (12 oz) pitted black cherries (frozen)

100 g (3.5 oz) granulated sugar

¼ cup (59 ml) Kirsch liqueur

Chocolate Mousse

¼ cup (59 ml) water

1½ tsp (5 g) powdered gelatin

340 g (12 oz) semisweet chocolate, chopped or chips

Pinch of salt

1 tsp vanilla extract

2 tbsp (24 g) granulated sugar (optional)

4 egg yolks

1½ cups (355 ml) plus ⅓ cup (79 ml) chilled whipping cream, divided

Cherry Filling

Place the water in a small bowl and sprinkle the gelatin over the surface. Let the gelatin bloom for 10 to 15 minutes.

Place the frozen black cherries and granulated sugar in a saucepan over medium heat and cook for 30 minutes, stirring frequently, to soften the cherries and create a cherry syrup. Fresh cherries will cook in a shorter time. Pour the cherries through a strainer to let the juices separate (do not squeeze or crush the whole cherries). Measure the cherry syrup, and add enough water to make ½ cup (118 ml) of liquid. Return the liquid and cherries to the saucepan, add the Kirsch liqueur and bloomed gelatin and cook over low heat to dissolve the gelatin (take care not to let the syrup boil). Pour the cherry mixture into a flat bowl and let it set in the fridge.

Chocolate Mousse

Line the bottom of a 3-inch (8-cm) tall, 8-inch (20-cm) wide springform pan with parchment paper. Line the sides with acetate paper or parchment paper.

Place the water in a small bowl and sprinkle the gelatin over the surface. Let the gelatin bloom for 10 to 15 minutes.

Place the semisweet chocolate in a heatproof bowl. Microwave in 30-second intervals to melt the chocolate, stirring in between. Add the bloomed gelatin, salt, vanilla, granulated sugar (if using, for a sweeter mousse), egg yolks and ⅓ cup (79 ml) of the cream and stir to form a smooth chocolate sauce. Microwave for 30 seconds (or more) to completely dissolve the gelatin and sugar in the chocolate. Let cool a bit (but don't let the chocolate set).

Place the remaining 1½ cups (355 ml) of cream in a cold metal bowl and whip with a mixer at medium speed until you get soft peaks. Add one-third of the cream to the cooled chocolate mixture and fold it in. Then fold in the rest of the cream in one or two additions. Spoon the chocolate mousse into the prepared pan, and let it set in the fridge for about an hour.

When the mousse layer has set, spoon the cherry filling on top with a ½- to ¾-inch (1.3- to 2-cm) gap around the edges (this cherry filling is quite soft, so it need not be intact—you can break it up into pieces if you like). Transfer to the fridge until the white chocolate mousse is ready.

(continued)

White Chocolate Mousse

¼ cup (59 ml) water

1½ tsp (5 g) powdered gelatin

226 g (8 oz) white chocolate, chopped or chips

Pinch of salt

1 tsp vanilla extract

3 egg yolks

1¼ cups (296 ml) chilled whipping cream, divided

Stabilized Kirsch Whipped Cream

2 tbsp (30 ml) water

½ tsp powdered gelatin

1 cup (236 ml) plus ½ tbsp (7 ml) chilled whipping cream, divided

2 tbsp (30 ml) Kirsch liqueur

¼ cup (33 g) confectioners' sugar

To Decorate

Shaved chocolate

White Chocolate Mousse

Place the water in a small bowl and sprinkle the gelatin over the surface. Let it bloom for 10 to 15 minutes.

Place the white chocolate in a heatproof bowl. Microwave in 30-second intervals to melt the chocolate, stirring in between. When the chocolate has melted, add the bloomed gelatin, salt, vanilla, egg yolks and ¼ cup (59 ml) of the cream and stir to form a smooth chocolate sauce. Microwave in 30-second intervals to completely dissolve the gelatin and chocolate. Let cool (but don't let the chocolate set).

Place the remaining 1 cup (236 ml) of cream in a cold metal bowl, and whip with a mixer at medium speed until you get soft peaks. Add one-third of the cream to the cooled chocolate mix and fold it in. Then fold in the rest of the cream in one or two additions.

Spoon the white chocolate mousse over the chocolate and cherry layers in the prepared pan, and let it set in the freezer overnight.

Stabilized Kirsch Whipped Cream

Place the water in a small bowl and sprinkle the gelatin over the surface evenly. Set aside for 10 to 15 minutes to let the gelatin bloom. Microwave the bloomed gelatin in 10-second intervals, stirring in between, until the gelatin has completely dissolved (take care not to let the gelatin boil).

Add 1 cup (236 ml) of the chilled whipping cream, Kirsch liqueur and confectioners' sugar to a cold bowl. Whisk with the whisk attachment at medium speed. Add the remaining ½ tablespoon (7 ml) of cream to the hot, dissolved gelatin mix. Add this gradually to the cream that is being whipped (being careful to pour it near the whisk, so that the gelatin gets mixed in with the cream immediately!). Whisk gently until you get stiff peaks.

Place the cream in a pastry bag with a large open star or closed star tip. Use immediately.

Decorate

Gently release the frozen mousse cake from the springform pan and remove the acetate paper or parchment paper. Smooth the sides if needed, using a warm spatula. Transfer the frozen mousse cake to a serving tray and place the cake in the fridge or on the counter to thaw slightly. The cake is easier to cut into when it is firm.

Pipe a whipped cream border on top and fill the center with chocolate shavings. Refrigerate until ready to serve.

Panettone Trifle Cake

Panettone is one of my favorite things to binge eat during Christmas season. I love making French toast or bread pudding with it as well. This secret-layer cake is like a bread pudding, a summer berry pudding and a trifle all in one. It looks quite rustic from the outside, but tucked away on the inside is an explosion of juicy berry deliciousness.

Makes one 8—inch (2∅—cm) cake

Panettone Loaf

907 g (32 oz) store-bought panettone loaf

Mixed Berry Layer

455 g (16 oz) frozen mixed berries like raspberries, strawberries, blueberries and blackberries, thawed

100 g (3.5 oz) granulated sugar

¼ cup (59 ml) port wine

¼ cup (59 ml) water

1 tsp powdered gelatin

226 g (8 oz) fresh mixed berries

Pastry Cream Layer

2 tbsp (30 ml) water

1 tsp powdered gelatin

2 eggs

1 tbsp (9 g) cornflour (cornstarch)

1 cup (236 ml) half-and-half (or ½ cup [118 ml] milk and ½ cup [118 ml] cream)

1 tbsp (15 ml) vanilla bean paste

Pinch of salt

70 g (2.5 oz) granulated sugar

1 cup (236 ml) chilled whipped cream

Panettone Loaf

Cut into the panettone loaf in a circle from the bottom, leaving a ½- to 1-inch (1.3- to 2.5-cm) border along the edges and the top, hollowing out the core of the loaf to make a bowl. It's important that you remove this core in one piece.

Slice off a ½-inch (1.3-cm) slice from the bottom of the core that you removed (we will be using this slice to seal the stuffed panettone loaf later). You can tear the rest of the core that you removed into big chunks. Set aside. (See photo on the next page.)

Mixed Berry Layer

Combine the berries and granulated sugar in a bowl. Cover and let the berries macerate overnight in the fridge (you will end up with sugar, berry syrup and softened fruits). Add the port and gently mix to combine.

Place the water in a heatproof bowl. Sprinkle the gelatin over the water and let it bloom for 10 to 15 minutes. Microwave the bloomed gelatin in 10-second intervals until the gelatin dissolves (take care not to let the mixture boil). Add the gelatin to the berry mixture and stir gently to combine. Fold in the fresh berries and set aside to cool and thicken slightly.

Pastry Cream Layer

Place the water in a bowl. Sprinkle the gelatin over the water and let it bloom for 10 to 15 minutes.

In another bowl, whisk the eggs and cornflour to form a smooth paste.

Place the half-and-half, vanilla bean paste, salt and granulated sugar in a saucepan and heat to melt the sugar. When it starts to steam, add some of the hot liquid to the eggs (while whisking) to temper the eggs. Add the tempered eggs back into the liquid and cook over medium heat, stirring continuously for 6 to 10 minutes, until thickened. Remove from the heat and add the bloomed gelatin. Whisk to dissolve the gelatin completely. Let the custard cool while whisking occasionally.

In a separate bowl, whisk the chilled cream on medium speed until you have soft peaks. Fold the whipped cream into the custard in two additions until just combined.

Vanilla Whipped Cream

1 cup (236 ml) chilled whipping cream

¼ cup (33 g) confectioners' sugar

2 tsp (10 ml) vanilla extract

To Decorate

Extra fresh berries

Extra macerated berries

Vanilla Whipped Cream

When ready to serve, in a bowl, whisk the chilled cream with the confectioners' sugar and vanilla on medium speed until you have soft peaks.

Decorate

Get all the components ready—hollowed-out panettone loaf, panettone bread chunks, ½-inch (1.3-cm) thick panettone slice, berry mixture and pastry cream. Scoop some of the berry juice from the bowl of berries and drizzle in the bottom of the hollowed-out panettone; layer one-third of the berries on the bottom. Top with a layer of pastry cream. Next, add a layer of panettone bread chunks. Drizzle some berry juice on top. Next, add another one-third of berries, pastry cream and bread chunks. Press down gently. Drizzle some berry juice on top. For the final layer, add the remaining berries to fill the panettone loaf (you might not use all of the berries). Drizzle the berry juice on the ½-inch (1.3-cm) thick panettone slice and "seal" the stuffed panettone with it. Triple wrap the panettone with plastic wrap as tightly as you can. Flip it over and store in the fridge for a few hours (or up to 24 hours), to set. The panettone loaf will stay for a couple of days in the fridge.

Unwrap the panettone, place on a platter and spread the vanilla whipped cream on top. Decorate with fresh berries and drizzle with any of the remaining macerated berries or berry juice.

*See photo on page 138.

Ice Cream Cakes

These ice cream cakes are going to be your best friend come summer. I've made it easier by using store-bought ice cream. You can use vanilla ice cream as a canvas on which to build different flavor combinations. And you can find inspiration anywhere, from a candy bar (Rocky Road Ice Cream Cake [page 165]) to cocktails (Piña Colada Ice Cream Cake [page 166]) to classics (Apple Pie Ice Cream Cake [page 182]). You can experiment with fudge layers, brownie layers and cake layers for added texture and flavor. My favorite is one that adds some crunch to the ice cream—like Pumpkin Pie Butter Pecan Praline Ice Cream Cake (page 177)! Utterly addictive.

Ice cream cakes are also easy to decorate with stabilized whipped cream and ice cream sundae sauces. My favorite ice cream sauces are chocolate fudge sauce, caramel sauce and butterscotch sauce—they are the perfect complement to creamy ice cream.

I hope these recipes inspire you to create your own favorite combinations with secret layers to surprise your friends, family and guests this summer!

Peanut Butter and Jelly
Ice Cream Cake

I had never had a PB&J sandwich until I was an adult! So I've got a lot of lost time and snacking to catch up on, and now I love coming up with ways to incorporate that quintessential PB&J flavor combo into various desserts. This ice cream cake is an example. What makes it even better is that it's topped with toast-infused whipped cream. That's toast-flavored whipped cream—how awesome is that? I like using it in a variety of recipes because it adds a really unique flavor, but I think it's best showcased in sweetened whipped cream.

Makes one 8–inch (20–cm) cake

Peanut Butter Blondie

115 g (4 oz) unsalted butter

115 g (4 oz) peanut butter (creamy or crunchy)

½ tsp salt

200 g (7 oz) brown sugar

2 eggs

1 tsp vanilla extract

150 g (5.3 oz) all-purpose flour

Raspberry Peanut Ice Cream

1.4 L (48 oz [3 pints]) vanilla ice cream, softened

340 g (12 oz) raspberries (thawed from frozen or fresh)

185 g (6.5 oz) Nutter Butter cookies (or similar type of peanut cookie), chopped into small pieces

Peanut Butter Blondie

Preheat the oven to 350°F (180°C). Butter an 8-inch (20-cm) wide, 3-inch (8-cm) tall pan. Line the bottom with parchment paper and dust the sides with flour.

Combine the butter, peanut butter, salt and brown sugar in a heatproof bowl and melt in 30-second intervals in the microwave. Stir to form a smooth butter-sugar mix. Set aside to let cool slightly.

When the sugar mixture has cooled, add the eggs, one at a time, whisking well after each addition. Stir in the vanilla. Fold in the flour.

Pour the batter into the prepared pan and bake for 15 to 20 minutes (the blondie should be soft and fudgy in the middle).

Remove from the oven and let cool. Remove from the pan and refrigerate, so it will be firmer and easier to handle when assembling the cake.

Raspberry Peanut Ice Cream

Let the vanilla ice cream soften for a few minutes. Puree the raspberries in a blender or food processor and fold it in to the vanilla ice cream. Fold in the chopped peanut butter cookies as well.

(continued)

Peanut Butter and Jelly
Ice Cream Cake (cont.)

Stabilized Toast–Flavored Whipped Cream

6 slices white bread

4 cups (946 ml) plus 1 tbsp (15 ml) chilled whipping cream, divided

¼ cup (59 ml) water

1½ tsp (7 g) powdered gelatin

½ cup (65 g) confectioners' sugar

To Decorate

Melted chocolate

Extra Nutter Butter cookies (or similar type of peanut butter cookie)

Raspberries

Peanuts

Stabilized Toast–Flavored Whipped Cream

Preheat the oven to 350°F (180°C).

Place the slices of bread on a baking tray and toast until they turn dark brown (but do not burn), about 10 minutes. Flip them over and toast for a 5 minutes longer, until they are dark brown all over. Remove from the oven and roughy break up the bread slices into halves or quarters.

Place 4 cups (946 ml) of the cream in a saucepan and then put the pieces of toast in the cream. Bring the cream to a simmer over medium heat. Stir gently and frequently as it heats up (taking care not to let the saturated pieces of toast break up further). As soon as the cream starts to steam, turn off the heat and let the toast steep until the cream cools down to room temperature, 20 to 30 minutes.

Next, pour the cream and toast into a nut milk bag and squeeze out as much of the liquid as possible (you'll likely end up with 2 to 2½ cups [473 to 592 ml] of toast-infused cream). Refrigerate the cream in a bowl or bottle until chilled. (You will only be using 2 cups [473 ml] of the cream for this recipe; you can use the leftover for making French toast, custard or any recipe that calls for cream.)

Place the water in a small bowl and evenly sprinkle the gelatin over it. Set aside for 10 to 15 minutes to let the gelatin bloom. Microwave the bloomed gelatin in 10-second intervals, stirring in between, until the gelatin is completely dissolved (take care not to let the gelatin boil).

Add 2 cups (473 ml) of the chilled toast-infused cream and the confectioners' sugar to a cold bowl. Whisk with the whisk attachment of your mixer on medium speed. Add the remaining 1 tablespoon (15 ml) of chilled cream to the hot, dissolved gelatin mix. Add this gradually to the cream that is being whipped (being careful to pour it near the whisk, so that the gelatin gets mixed in with the cream immediately!). Whisk gently on medium speed, until you get stiff peaks. Transfer to a pastry bag with a star tip. Use immediately.

Decorate

Line the bottom of an 8-inch (20-cm) springform pan with parchment paper and the sides with parchment paper or acetate paper. Place the peanut butter blondie at the bottom of the pan. Then evenly spread the raspberry peanut ice cream on top to create a flat surface. Return the ice cream cake to the freezer until frozen.

Using a little melted chocolate, stick Nutter Butter cookies on the sides of the cake. Pipe swirls of toast-flavored whipped cream on top and decorate with raspberries and peanuts.

Cookies and Cream
Brownie Ice Cream Cake

If you love cookies and cream ice cream, then this is for you! An Oreo-stuffed brownie layer is smothered with cookies and cream ice cream, then topped with chocolate fudge sauce and more Oreos!

Makes one 8–inch (20–cm) cake

Oreo–Stuffed Brownie Layer

115 g (4 oz) bittersweet chocolate, chopped

115 g (4 oz) unsalted butter

142 g (5 oz) granulated sugar

¼ tsp salt

1 tsp vanilla extract

2 eggs

85 g (3 oz) all-purpose flour

10 Oreo cookies

Chocolate Fudge Sauce

⅔ cup (158 ml) heavy or whipping cream

3 tbsp (44 ml) corn syrup

50 g (1.7 oz) granulated sugar

70 g (2.5 oz) brown sugar

30 g (1 oz) unsweetened cocoa powder

¼ tsp kosher salt

200 g (7 oz) semisweet chocolate, chopped or chips

2 tbsp (29 g) unsalted butter

Oreo–Stuffed Brownie Layer

Preheat the oven to 350°F (180°C). Butter an 8-inch (20-cm) wide, 3-inch (8-cm) tall pan. Line the bottom with parchment paper and dust the sides with flour.

In a heatproof bowl, melt the chocolate and butter in the microwave in 30-second intervals, stirring in between to prevent the chocolate from burning. Let the chocolate-butter mix cool.

Add the granulated sugar, salt and vanilla, and whisk to combine. Next, add the eggs, one at a time, whisking well after each addition. Fold in the flour until just combined.

Pour two-thirds of the batter into the prepared pan and spread it evenly. Place the Oreo cookies in one layer over the brownie batter and spread the remaining brownie batter over the cookies. Bake for 20 minutes.

Remove from the oven and let cool completely. Remove from the pan and refrigerate the brownie layer to make it easier to handle for the ice cream cake.

Chocolate Fudge Sauce

Place the cream, corn syrup, granulated sugar, brown sugar, cocoa powder and salt in a saucepan over medium-high heat. Whisk to melt the sugar and cocoa powder. Bring it to a boil. Reduce the heat to medium and let it simmer for about 5 minutes. Remove from the heat and stir in the chopped chocolate and butter until melted. Set aside to let the fudge sauce cool.

(continued)

Cookies and Cream Brownie
Ice Cream Cake (cont.)

Ice Cream Layer

1.4 L (48 oz [3 pints]) cookies and cream ice cream

20 Oreo cookies

1 cup (236 ml) milk

Stabilized Whipped Cream

2 tbsp (30 ml) water

¾ tsp powdered gelatin

1 cup (236 ml) plus ½ tbsp (7 ml) chilled whipping cream, divided

2 tbsp (16 g) confectioners' sugar

To Decorate

Crushed Oreos

Ice Cream Layer

Soften the cookies and cream ice cream. Line the bottom of the 8-inch (20-cm) springform pan with parchment paper, and line the sides with parchment paper or acetate paper.

Place the refrigerated brownie layer at the bottom of the prepared pan. Spread one-third of the cookies and cream ice cream over the refrigerated brownie layer. Spread a thin layer of chocolate fudge sauce. Dunk Oreo cookies in milk for just a couple of seconds and layer the cookies on top of the fudge sauce. Repeat the layers one more time, and finally top the cake with the remaining cookies and cream ice cream. Spread the layer evenly to create a flat surface and top with some of the crushed Oreo cookies. Freeze the cake to let it completely set.

Stabilized Whipped Cream

When ready to assemble, place the water in a small bowl and evenly sprinkle the gelatin over it. Set aside for 10 to 15 minutes to let the gelatin bloom.

Microwave the bloomed gelatin in 10-second intervals, stirring in between, until the gelatin is completely dissolved (take care not to let the gelatin boil).

Add 1 cup (236 ml) of the chilled whipping cream and the confectioners' sugar to a cold bowl. Whisk with the whisk attachment of your hand mixer on medium speed. Add the remaining ½ tablespoon (7 ml) of chilled cream to the hot, dissolved gelatin mix. Add this gradually to the cream that is being whipped (being careful to pour it near the whisk, so that the gelatin gets mixed in with the cream immediately!). Whisk gently until you get stiff peaks. Transfer to a pastry bag with a star tip. Use immediately.

Decorate

When the ice cream cake has set, pour the remaining fudge sauce over the top. When the fudge sauce has set, pipe whipped cream swirls on top and decorate with the remaining crushed Oreos. Return to the freezer until you're ready to serve the cake. Let the ice cream cake soften for about 5 minutes to make it easier to slice.

Rocky Road
Ice Cream Cake

Rocky road is my weakness. There used to be a little shop in Brisbane, Australia, that sold the best rocky road candy I have ever tasted in my life! The perfect rocky road doesn't need anything else other than chocolate, raspberry, marshmallows and peanuts—and that's exactly what you get in this decadent ice cream cake.

Makes one 8-inch (20-cm) cake

Peanut Butter Chocolate Fudge

340 g (12 oz) smooth peanut butter

¼ cup (59 ml) whipping cream

340 g (12 oz) milk chocolate, chopped or chips

¼ tsp salt

Rocky Road Ice Cream

226 g (8 oz) raspberries

57 g (2 oz) sugar

1.4 L (48 oz [3 pints]) chocolate ice cream

1 heaped cup (115 g) marshmallow crème

Brownie Layer

115 g (4 oz) bittersweet chocolate, chopped

115 g (4 oz) unsalted butter

142 g (5 oz) sugar

¼ tsp salt

1 tsp vanilla extract

2 eggs

85 g (3 oz) all-purpose flour

To Decorate

1–2 cups (100–200 g) marshmallow crème

Fresh raspberries

Chopped peanuts

Chocolate shavings

Peanut Butter Chocolate Fudge

Line the bottom of an 8-inch (20-cm) springform pan with parchment paper and line the sides with acetate paper or parchment paper.

Melt the peanut butter, cream and chocolate in a heatproof bowl in 30-second intervals in the microwave (or over a pan of simmering water). Add the salt and mix until nice and smooth. Pour the mixture into the bottom of the prepared pan and refrigerate until the ice cream layer is ready.

Rocky Road Ice Cream

Puree the raspberries and sugar in a food processor or blender to form a raspberry sauce. Soften the chocolate ice cream a bit. Then place the chocolate ice cream in a bowl and dollop the marshmallow crème over it. Fold in the crème to create marshmallow ripples. Next, add the raspberry puree and fold it in to create raspberry ripples in the ice cream.

Brownie Layer

Preheat the oven to 350°F (180°C). Butter an 8-inch (20-cm) wide, 3-inch (8-cm) tall pan. Line the bottom with parchment paper and dust the sides with flour.

Melt the chocolate and butter in a heatproof bowl in the microwave in 30-second intervals, stirring in between to prevent the chocolate from burning. Let the chocolate-butter mix cool. Add the sugar, salt and vanilla, and whisk to combine. Next, add the eggs, one at a time, whisking well after each addition. Fold in the flour until just combined. Pour the batter into the prepared pan and bake for 20 minutes. The brownie will be quite fudgy in the center, but this works better for an ice cream cake. Let the brownie layer cool, and cut it into small squares.

Decorate

Spread the rocky road ice cream layer over the peanut butter chocolate fudge layer. Place the cut-up brownie pieces on top of the rocky road ice cream layer, and press down to embed the brownie pieces in the ice cream. Freeze for at least a few hours, until the ice cream hardens.

When ready to serve, release the cake from the springform pan, and spread marshmallow crème over the top and about halfway down the sides. Using a blowtorch, caramelize the marshmallow crème. Top the cake with fresh raspberries, chopped peanuts and chocolate shavings.

Piña Colada
Ice Cream Cake

Who doesn't love a good piña colada cocktail on a summer day? Psst, who am I kidding? Even on a cold, rainy, dreary day, a piña colada would be irresistible to me. This summery ice cream does not have any alcohol, but it does feature that awesome coconut and pineapple one-two punch. The meringue layer adds a nice crunch, too. It's an ice cream cake that your whole family can enjoy.

Makes one 8–inch (20–cm) cake

Coconut Meringue Layer

100 g (3.5 oz) sugar

½ tbsp (5 g) cornflour (cornstarch)

2 egg whites, at room temperature

Pinch of cream of tartar

Pinch of salt

1 tsp vanilla extract

50 g (1.7 oz) desiccated coconut

Coconut and Pineapple Ice Cream

1.4 L (48 oz [3 pints]) coconut ice cream

455 g (16 oz) pineapple, cored (thawed from frozen or fresh)

Coconut Meringue Layer

Preheat the oven to 250°F (120°C). Line a baking sheet with parchment paper and draw a 7-inch (18-cm) circle on it. Turn the parchment paper over, so that the drawn circle is facing the bottom but you can still see the lines through the paper.

In a dry food processor, process the sugar until you have superfine sugar granules. Add the cornflour and mix to combine.

Place the egg whites in a clean, dry metal bowl of your stand mixer (you can use a hand mixer or a stand mixer for this, but it'll be easier in a stand mixer). Add the cream of tartar and salt. Whisk on high speed until you have soft peaks. Lower the speed to medium, and gradually add the sugar while continuously whisking the egg whites. Once all the sugar has been added, scrape down the sides of the bowl to get any sugar that may have stuck to the sides. Whisk the egg whites on medium-high speed for another 5 to 7 minutes, until all the sugar crystals have completely dissolved. (You can check if the sugar has dissolved by rubbing some of the egg whites between your fingers every couple of minutes—if the sugar has dissolved, the egg whites will feel smooth; if it feels gritty, the meringue is not ready yet.) Add the vanilla and coconut and whisk for a few seconds on high speed to combine.

Spoon the meringue into the drawn circle and spread it evenly to fill the circle. Bake for 2 hours. Turn off the oven and let the meringue cool completely inside the oven, with the oven door left ajar. The meringue can be kept in an airtight container until needed.

Coconut and Pineapple Ice Cream

When the meringue layer is ready to be topped, thaw the coconut ice cream a bit.

In a food processor or blender, process the pineapple until it becomes a smooth pulp. Add the pineapple to the softened coconut ice cream and fold to combine (it doesn't have to be completely mixed through—ripples are OK).

(continued)

Stabilized Whipped Cream

3 tbsp (44 ml) water

1½ tsp (5 g) powdered gelatin

2 cups (473 ml) plus 1 tbsp (15 ml) chilled whipping cream, divided

½ cup (65 g) confectioners' sugar

1 tsp vanilla extract

To Decorate

Maraschino cherries

Pineapple pieces

Toasted coconut flakes

Stabilized Whipped Cream

When ready to serve the cake, place the water in a small heatproof bowl and evenly sprinkle the gelatin over it. Set aside for 10 to 15 minutes to let the gelatin bloom. Microwave the bloomed gelatin in 10-second intervals, stirring in between, until the gelatin is completely dissolved (it's important that you don't let the gelatin boil).

Add 2 cups (473 ml) of the chilled whipping cream, confectioners' sugar and vanilla to a cold bowl. Whisk with the whisk attachment of your hand mixer on medium speed. Add the remaining 1 tablespoon (15 ml) of chilled cream to the hot, dissolved gelatin mix. Add this gradually to the cream that is being whipped (being careful to pour it near the whisk, so that the gelatin gets mixed in with the cream immediately!). Whisk on medium speed until you get stiff peaks. Transfer to a pastry bag with a star tip. Use immediately.

Assemble

Line the bottom of an 8-inch (20-cm) springform pan with parchment paper. Line the sides with parchment paper or acetate paper.

Place the meringue layer on the bottom of the springform pan. Top the meringue layer with the softened coconut and pineapple ice cream. Return it to the freezer to let it set.

Decorate

Once the ice cream cake is frozen, remove it from the springform pan and quickly frost the cake with the stabilized whipped cream (this needs to be done quickly because the cream will set and make it hard to spread). Pipe whipped cream swirls on the top and top the cake with maraschino cherries, pineapple slices and toasted coconut flakes. Keep the cake in the freezer until you're ready to serve. This cake is best served within 24 to 48 hours.

Funfetti Explosion
Birthday Ice Cream Cake

This cake looks like a funfetti cannon exploded all over it. Kids love rainbow colors and funfetti, so it'll be perfect for a summer birthday party! A fudgy blondie layer is packed with funfetti and topped with a cake batter–flavored funfetti ice cream layer. Top it with some sparklers to complete the look.

Makes one 8–inch (20–cm) cake

Funfetti Blondie Layer

170 g (6 oz) unsalted butter

½ tsp salt

250 g (8.8 oz) brown sugar

2 eggs

1 tsp vanilla extract

175 g (6.2 oz) all-purpose flour

½ cup (113 g) funfetti (rainbow) sprinkles

Funfetti Cake Batter Ice Cream Layer

¼ cup (59 ml) whipping cream

¼ cup (61 g) milk powder

1 tsp vanilla extract

1.9 L (64 oz [4 pints]) vanilla ice cream, softened

1½ cups (339 g) funfetti (rainbow) sprinkles

Funfetti Blondie Layer

Preheat the oven to 350°F (180°C). Butter an 8-inch (20-cm) wide, 3-inch (8-cm) tall springform pan. Line the bottom with parchment paper and dust the sides with flour.

Melt the butter, salt and brown sugar in a heatproof bowl in 30-second intervals in the microwave. Stir to form a smooth butter-sugar mixture. Set aside to let cool slightly.

Once the butter-sugar mix has cooled, add the eggs, one at a time, whisking well after each addition. Stir in the vanilla and the flour. Fold in the funfetti sprinkles.

Pour the batter into the prepared pan and bake for 25 to 30 minutes (the blondie should still be soft and fudgy in the middle). Let the blondie cool in the pan. When it has cooled, line the sides with parchment paper or acetate paper. Refrigerate the blondie layer until the ice cream is ready.

Funfetti Cake Batter Ice Cream Layer

Microwave the cream until it's warm, but not hot. Add the milk powder and dissolve it completely. Add the vanilla and stir to combine. Let cool.

Place the softened vanilla ice cream in a bowl, add the cooled milk powder mixture and stir to combine. Fold in the funfetti sprinkles. Spread the ice cream over the funfetti blondie.

Place the ice cream in the freezer until it freezes and hardens completely. This makes it easier to frost the cake quickly.

(continued)

Stabilized Whipped Cream

½ cup (118 ml) water

3¾ tsp (19 g) powdered gelatin

5 cups (1 L) plus 1–2 tbsp (15–30 ml) chilled whipping cream, divided

1 cup (130 g) confectioners' sugar

Red, orange, yellow, green, blue and purple gel food coloring

To Decorate

Funfetti sprinkles

M&M's® candies

Stabilized Whipped Cream

Place the water in a small bowl and evenly sprinkle the gelatin over it. Set aside for 10 to 15 minutes to let the gelatin bloom. Microwave the bloomed gelatin in 10-second intervals, stirring in between, until the gelatin is completely dissolved (making sure that the gelatin does not boil).

Add 5 cups (1.2 L) of the chilled whipping cream and confectioners' sugar to a cold bowl. Whisk with the whisk attachment of your hand mixer on medium speed. Add the remaining 1 to 2 tablespoons (15 to 30 ml) of chilled cream to the hot, dissolved gelatin and stir to temper the gelatin. Add this gradually to the cream that is being whipped (being careful to pour it near the whisk, so that the gelatin gets mixed in with the cream immediately!). Whisk gently until you get soft peaks that still hold their shape. Use immediately.

Work quickly to frost the frozen ice cream cake. Divide the whipped cream into 7 portions, then combine two to make one larger portion (so that you have 5 small portions and 1 double portion). Color the small portions with red, orange, yellow, green and blue gel food coloring. Color the double portion with purple.

Decorate

Remove the completely frozen funfetti ice cream cake from the freezer, and unmold from the springform pan. Spread the whipped cream on the sides of the cake to create a rainbow pattern—either rainbow patches, or rainbow ombre stripes—starting with red at the bottom and purple at the top edge and on the top of the cake. You can use the leftover whipped cream to pipe rainbow swirls on top of the cake as well.

Sprinkle some funfetti sprinkles and M&M's on top (in the center). Return the cake to the freezer until you're ready to serve.

Lemon Meringue Bombe Alaska

Everyone loves a good lemon meringue pie. But come summer, this ice cream cake version will be everyone's new favorite! Rich, tangy lemon curd is swirled into ice cream with layers of buttery shortbread cookies. The meringue frosting is sweet and marshmallowy, just like meringue pie topping.

Makes one 8-inch (20-cm) cake

Lemon Curd Ice Cream

1 cup (236 ml) lemon juice (from 10-12 lemons)

200 g (7 oz) sugar

114 g (4 oz) unsalted butter

2 tsp (6 g) cornflour (cornstarch)

Zest of 4-5 lemons

6 eggs

1.4 L (48 oz [3 pints]) good-quality vanilla ice cream

Shortbread Cookie Layer

20-25 shortbread cookies (or enough for 2 shortbread layers)

1 cup (236 ml) warm milk

Meringue Layer

5 egg whites

200 g (7 oz) sugar

Pinch of salt

Pinch of cream of tartar

2 tsp (10 ml) vanilla extract

To Decorate

Lemon slices

Lemon Curd Ice Cream

This can be made ahead of time. Place the lemon juice, sugar, butter, cornflour and lemon zest in a saucepan. Whisk to combine. Heat over medium heat to dissolve the sugar. Place the eggs in a bowl and whisk to combine. When the sugar has dissolved, add the warm lemon mixture to the eggs gradually, whisking continuously to prevent the eggs from scrambling. Return the lemon-egg mixture to the saucepan and heat over medium heat while whisking continuously to thicken the mixture (take care not to let the eggs scramble). When the mixture has thickened, remove from the heat and let cool completely. Whisk frequently to prevent a skin from forming on the surface of the lemon curd. Keep the lemon curd in the fridge to make sure it is cold before adding to the ice cream.

Soften the vanilla ice cream and scoop the ice cream into a bowl. Add the lemon curd to the ice cream and fold it in. Keep the ice cream in the freezer until ready to use.

Shortbread Cookie Layer

Line the bottom of an 8-inch (20-cm) springform pan with parchment paper and the sides with parchment or acetate paper.

Add one-third of the lemon curd ice cream to the bottom of the pan (a fairly thin layer), and spread it evenly. Dip the shortbread cookies in the warm milk (do not let the cookie get too soggy) and place on top of the ice cream layer to completely cover. Top with another one-third of the ice cream. Repeat with another layer of shortbread cookies. Top with the remaining lemon curd ice cream and freeze until firm (overnight).

Meringue Layer

Bring a little water to a boil in a saucepan. Lower the heat to bring it to a simmer. Combine the egg whites, sugar, salt and cream of tartar in a clean, dry metal bowl. Place the metal bowl over the simmering water (be careful not to let the water mix with your egg whites) and whisk continuously to dissolve the sugar in the egg whites, 5 to 10 minutes.

When the sugar has completely dissolved, remove the egg whites from the double boiler and whisk them on high speed, using a whisk attachment in a hand mixer or stand mixer, until doubled in volume, the egg whites are thick and glossy and the bowl is cool to the touch. Add the vanilla and whisk for 1 minute. The meringue is now ready to be used immediately.

Decorate

When the ice cream cake is firm and ready to be served, release it from the pan and frost the cake with the meringue. Caramelize the sides using a culinary blowtorch. Decorate the cake with the lemon slices and serve immediately.

Chocolate Explosion
Ice Cream Cake

This EPIC chocolate-loaded ice cream cake is only for serious chocoholics. From the crisp meringue to the fudgy brownie, rich fudge sauce and fudgy ice cream—everything is chocolate in this cake. Plus, it's decorated with chocolate bark that pops and fizzles in your mouth! Given all that, I think it's fair to call this the Chocolate Explosion Ice Cream Cake. The fudge sauce makes about 3 cups (708 ml), and you won't be using all of it for this recipe—unless you want to, of course!

Makes one 8—inch (20—cm) cake

Chocolate Meringue Layer

100 g (3.5 oz) granulated sugar

½ tbsp (5 g) cornflour (cornstarch)

2 egg whites

Pinch of salt

Pinch of cream of tartar

1 tsp vanilla extract

1 tbsp (7 g) cocoa powder

Chocolate Brownie Layer

115 g (4 oz) bittersweet chocolate, chopped

115 g (4 oz) unsalted butter

142 g (5 oz) granulated sugar

¼ tsp salt

1 tsp vanilla extract

2 eggs

70 g (2.5 oz) all-purpose flour

Chocolate Meringue Layer

This can be made a day ahead. Preheat the oven to 250°F (120°C). Line a baking sheet with parchment paper and draw a 7-inch (18-cm) circle on it. Turn the parchment paper over, so that the drawn circle is facing the bottom but you can still see the lines through the paper.

In a dry food processor, process the sugar until you have superfine sugar granules. Add the cornflour and mix to combine.

Place the egg whites in a clean, dry metal bowl of your stand mixer (you can use a hand mixer or a stand mixer for this, but it'll be easier in a stand mixer). Add the salt and cream of tartar. Whisk on high speed until you have soft peaks. Lower the speed to medium and gradually add the superfine sugar while continuously whisking the egg whites. When all the sugar has been added, scrape down the sides of the bowl to get any sugar that may have stuck to the sides. Whisk the egg whites on medium-high speed for another 5 to 7 minutes, until all the sugar crystals have completely dissolved. (You can check if the sugar has dissolved by rubbing some of the egg whites between your fingers every couple of minutes—if the sugar has dissolved, the egg whites will feel smooth; if it feels gritty, the meringue is not ready yet.) Add the vanilla and cocoa powder and whisk for a few seconds to combine.

Spoon the meringue inside the drawn circle and spread it evenly to fill the circle. Bake for 1½ to 2 hours, until the meringue is dry. Turn off the oven and let the meringues cool completely inside the oven, with the oven door left ajar, at least 2 hours.

The meringue can be kept in an airtight container until needed.

Chocolate Brownie Layer

This can be made a day ahead as well. Preheat the oven to 350°F (180°C). Butter an 8-inch (20-cm) wide, 3-inch (8-cm) tall springform pan. Line the bottom with parchment paper and dust the sides with flour.

Melt the chocolate and butter in the microwave in 30-second intervals, stirring in between to prevent the chocolate from burning. Let the chocolate-butter mix cool.

Add the granulated sugar, salt and vanilla, and whisk to combine. Next, add the eggs, one at a time, whisking well after each addition. Fold in the flour until just combined.

Pour the batter into the prepared pan and bake for 20 minutes (the center will be quite fudgy, but that is OK because this will be frozen later). Let the brownie cool, and refrigerate to make it easier to handle.

(continued)

Chocolate Explosion
Ice Cream Cake (cont.)

Chocolate Fudge Sauce

1⅓ cups (316 ml) whipping cream

⅓ cup (79 ml) corn syrup

½ cup (96 g) granulated sugar

⅔ cup (132 g) packed dark brown sugar

½ cup (56 g) good-quality unsweetened cocoa powder

½ tsp kosher salt

400 g (14 oz) semisweet chocolate, chopped or chips

57 g (2 oz) unsalted butter

Chocolate Popping Candy Bark

225 g (8 oz) milk chocolate or semisweet chocolate, melted

⅓ cup (77 g) popping candy (neutral or cocoa butter coated)

Melted white chocolate or sprinkles (optional)

Chocolate Fudge Ice Cream

1.4 L (48 oz [3 pints]) chocolate ice cream

½ recipe of chocolate fudge sauce (above) or 1–1½ cups (227–341 g) store-bought fudge sauce

Chocolate Fudge Sauce

Place the whipping cream, corn syrup, granulated sugar, dark brown sugar, cocoa powder and salt in a saucepan over medium-high heat and whisk to melt the sugar and cocoa powder. Bring the mixture to a boil (it'll bubble up). Reduce the heat to medium and let it simmer for about 5 minutes. Remove from the heat and stir in the chopped chocolate and butter until glossy and smooth. Let the chocolate fudge sauce cool before using it.

Chocolate Popping Candy Bark

Melt the chocolate in the microwave in 30-second intervals, stirring in between. Allow the chocolate to cool a bit. (If the chocolate is too hot when you add the popping candy, especially uncoated popping candy, it can cause the popping candy to melt and not pop properly, which takes all the fun out of popping candy!)

Add the popping candy to the cooled melted chocolate and spread the chocolate on a piece of acetate paper or parchment paper, being careful not to crush the popping candy. Drizzle white chocolate or sprinkles on top, if desired. Let the chocolate set and then break it up into pieces. Use a warm knife to make cutting easier. Store in an airtight container.

Chocolate Fudge Ice Cream

Soften the chocolate ice cream. Drizzle on the chocolate fudge sauce and fold it in to create a fudge ripple in the ice cream.

Decorate

Line the bottom of an 8-inch (20-cm) springform pan, and line the sides with parchment paper or acetate paper. Place the chocolate meringue layer at the bottom. Top the meringue with half of the softened chocolate fudge ice cream and spread it evenly. Next, place the chocolate brownie layer, followed by a layer of chocolate fudge sauce, followed by the remaining chocolate fudge ice cream. Spread evenly for a flat surface. Freeze the cake until firm.

When you're ready to serve, gently release the cake from the springform pan and top the cake with more fudge sauce and the chocolate popping candy bark. Keep the cake in the freezer until ready to serve.

Pumpkin Pie Butter Pecan Praline Ice Cream Cake

A taste of autumn in a summery ice cream cake. With layers of pumpkin pie, crunchy butter pecan praline, butter pecan ice cream and salted caramel sauce, this is one decadent, showstopping dessert!

Makes one 8—inch (20—cm) cake

Frozen Pumpkin Pie Layer

0.7 L (24 oz [1½ pints]) vanilla ice cream

230 g (8.1 oz) pumpkin puree

1 tsp pumpkin pie spice

115 g (4 oz) cream cheese, softened

Butter Pecan Praline

226 g (8 oz) unsalted butter

½ tsp kosher salt

226 g (8 oz) brown sugar

280 g (10 oz) graham crackers (about 32 squares)

200 g (7 oz) chopped pecans, divided

Butter Pecan Praline Ice Cream

½ recipe butter pecan praline (above), crushed

1.4 L (48 oz [3 pints]) vanilla ice cream, softened

Butterscotch Sauce

115 g (4 oz) unsalted butter

½ tsp kosher salt

115 g (4 oz) brown sugar

½ cup (118 ml) whipping cream

2 tsp (10 ml) vanilla extract

Frozen Pumpkin Pie Layer

Soften the vanilla ice cream. Place the pumpkin puree, pumpkin pie spice and cream cheese in a bowl. Mix until the mixture is smooth. Add to the vanilla ice cream and fold to combine well. Freeze until needed.

Butter Pecan Praline

Preheat the oven to 350°F (180°C). Line a 9 x 13-inch (23 x 33-cm) rimmed baking sheet with parchment paper.

Melt the butter, salt and brown sugar in a saucepan over medium heat. Whisk to form a smooth butter-sugar mix. Let the mix come to a boil and then let it boil for 2 to 3 minutes.

Place the graham crackers in a single layer on the prepared pan. Pour the hot butter-sugar mixture evenly over the crackers (you can use a spatula to evenly spread the mixture). Sprinkle two-thirds of the pecans over the crackers.

Transfer to the oven and bake for 10 minutes (you should see bubbling along the edges of the pan). Remove from the oven and let cool completely until the toffee hardens.

Break the graham cracker praline into squares. Place in a food processor and process to coarsely chop the graham crackers. Mix in the remaining one-third chopped pecans. Set aside until needed.

Butter Pecan Praline Ice Cream

Mix half of the butter pecan praline with the softened vanilla ice cream and return to the freezer.

Butterscotch Sauce

Melt the butter, salt and brown sugar in a saucepan over medium heat. Whisk to make sure you have a smooth sauce and the sugar is completely dissolved. Add the cream while whisking, and then reduce the heat to medium-low. Whisk to combine and bring the mixture to a boil. Let the butterscotch sauce boil gently for 10 to 15 minutes longer, stirring frequently, until it thickens. Stir in the vanilla. Let the butterscotch sauce cool completely before using. If the butterscotch sauce thickens too much, heat it gently with a splash of cream until you get the desired consistency.

(continued)

Pumpkin Pie Butter Pecan Praline Ice Cream Cake (cont.)

Whipped Cream

1 cup (236 ml) chilled whipping cream

¼ cup (33 g) confectioners' sugar

To Decorate

Pecan halves

Whipped Cream

Whisk the chilled cream and confectioners' sugar in a bowl on medium speed until you have stiff peaks. Place the whipped cream in a pastry bag with an open star tip. Use immediately.

Decorate

Line the bottom of an 8-inch (20-cm) springform pan with parchment paper and the sides with parchment paper or acetate paper.

Sprinkle half of the remaining butter pecan praline on the bottom of the cake pan. Top with half of the frozen pumpkin pie layer, followed by half of the butter pecan praline ice cream. Pour on half of the butterscotch sauce and swirl it into the ice cream. Repeat the layers with the remaining butter pecan praline, frozen pumpkin pie layer, pecan praline ice cream and swirled butterscotch sauce. Freeze the ice cream cake until firm.

Pipe the whipped cream over the ice cream cake and decorate with the pecan halves.

Afghan Fudge Hokey Pokey Ice Cream Cake

Hokey pokey ice cream (creamy vanilla ice cream with crunchy bits of honeycomb) is a New Zealand classic. I paired this ice cream with another Kiwi classic—Afghan cookies (biscuits) and a fudge layer for good measure.

Makes one 8-inch (20-cm) cake

Hokey Pokey Layer

1.4 L (48 oz [3 pints]) vanilla ice cream, softened

100 g (3.5 oz) chocolate-covered honeycomb bars, chopped into smaller chunks

Afghan Fudge Brownie Layer

115 g (4 oz) bittersweet chocolate, chopped

115 g (4 oz) unsalted butter

142 g (5 oz) granulated sugar

¼ tsp salt

1 tsp vanilla extract

2 eggs

85 g (3 oz) all-purpose flour

85 g (3 oz) cornflakes, coarsely crushed

56 g (2 oz) walnuts, chopped

Chocolate Fudge Sauce

⅔ cup (158 ml) heavy or whipping cream

3 tbsp (44 ml) corn syrup

50 g (1.7 oz) granulated sugar

70 g (2.5 oz) brown sugar

30 g (1 oz) unsweetened cocoa powder

¼ tsp kosher salt

200 g (7 oz) semisweet chocolate, chopped or chips

2 tbsp (29 g) unsalted butter

To Decorate

Walnut halves

Extra chocolate-covered honeycomb

Hokey Pokey Layer

Place the ice cream in a bowl and gently fold in the hokey pokey pieces.

Afghan Fudge Brownie Layer

Preheat the oven to 350°F (180°C). Butter an 8-inch (20-cm) wide, 3-inch (8-cm) tall pan. Line the bottom with parchment paper and dust the sides with flour.

Place the chocolate and butter in a heatproof bowl and melt in the microwave in 30-second intervals, stirring in between to prevent the chocolate from burning. Let the chocolate-butter mix cool. Add the granulated sugar, salt and vanilla, and whisk to combine. Next, add the eggs, one at a time, whisking well after each addition. Fold in the flour, crushed cornflakes and walnuts until just combined. Pour the batter into the prepared pan and bake for 15 to 20 minutes, until the edges are set but the middle is still runny. Refrigerate the brownie layer so it is easier to handle.

Chocolate Fudge Sauce

Place the cream, corn syrup, granulated sugar, brown sugar, cocoa powder and salt in a saucepan over medium-high heat. Whisk to melt the sugar and cocoa powder. Bring it to a boil. Reduce the heat to medium and let it simmer for about 5 minutes. Remove from the heat and stir in the chopped chocolate and butter. Set aside to let the fudge sauce cool.

Decorate

Line the bottom of an 8-inch (20-cm) springform pan with parchment paper and line the sides with parchment paper or acetate paper. Place the chilled brownie layer at the bottom of the pan.

Spread all of the hokey pokey ice cream on top. Freeze until hard.

When the ice cream cake is frozen, release the cake from the springform pan, and pour the chocolate fudge sauce on top. Return the cake to the freezer until ready to serve. Top the cake with walnut halves and extra honeycomb candy pieces just before serving.

Apple Pie
Ice Cream Cake

This is my decadent ice cream cake version of apple pie. Vanilla ice cream is mixed with apple pie filling and layered with seriously crunchy bits of caramel crumbs and caramel sauce.

Makes one 8–inch (20–cm) cake

"Pie Crust" Crumbs

226 g (8 oz) unsalted butter

½ tsp kosher salt

226 g (8 oz) brown sugar

280 g (10 oz) graham crackers (about 32 squares)

Apple Pie Ice Cream

595 g (21 oz) canned apple pie filling

1½ L (48 oz [3 pints]) good-quality vanilla ice cream

1 tsp ground cinnamon

Caramel Sauce

200 g (7 oz) granulated sugar

¼ cup (59 ml) water

2 tbsp (30 ml) corn syrup

½ cup (118 ml) whipping cream, warmed

Pinch of salt

1 tsp vanilla extract

To Decorate

Pie crust, store-bought or homemade (optional)

Egg wash (if using pie crust)

Extra apple pie filling

"Pie Crust" Crumbs

Preheat the oven to 350°F (180°C). Line a 9 x 13-inch (23 x 33-cm) sheet pan with parchment paper. Melt the butter, salt and brown sugar in a saucepan over medium heat. Whisk to form a smooth butter-sugar mix. Let the mix come to a boil and then let it boil for 2 to 3 minutes.

Place the graham crackers in a single layer on the prepared pan. Pour the hot butter-sugar mixture evenly over the crackers. Transfer to the oven and bake for 10 minutes (you should see bubbling along the edges of the pan). Remove from the oven and let cool completely until the toffee hardens. Break the graham cracker toffee into squares and place in a food processor to coarsely chop. Set aside until needed.

Apple Pie Ice Cream

Line the bottom of an 8-inch (20-cm) springform pan with parchment paper and line the sides with acetate or parchment paper. Chop the apple pie filling into smaller pieces. Soften the vanilla ice cream slightly. Add the apple pie filling and cinnamon, and fold in. Add half of the mixed ice cream to the prepared pan. Generously sprinkle a layer of the graham cracker toffee crumbs. Top it with the rest of the ice cream and cover with another generous layer of the graham cracker crumbs. Gently press it to create a flat surface. Freeze the ice cream cake overnight.

Caramel Sauce

Add the granulated sugar, water and corn syrup to a saucepan and swirl to combine. Cook over medium heat, letting the sugar dissolve without stirring the liquid, as this could crystallize the sugar. Let the sugar syrup come to a boil and gradually change color to a dark golden color. Slowly add the warm cream and salt, whisking continuously until you get a smooth, slightly thick caramel sauce, 2 to 5 minutes. Stir in the vanilla. Pour into a glass jar and set aside until needed. The caramel sauce should thicken as it cools down.

Decorate

Preheat the oven to 400°F (200°C). Line a baking sheet with parchment paper. Cut out different shapes from store-bought pie crust or shortcrust—flowers, leaves, etc. To create a braid circle (pie wreath), cut three ½-inch (1.2-cm) thick strips, pinch them together at the top and braid the strips. Pinch the bottom closed. Shape the braid into a 7½-inch (19-cm) diameter circle. Place on the prepared baking sheet. Brush the tops of all your pie crust decorations with egg wash and bake until golden brown, 5 to 10 minutes. Check on the pie crust every few minutes to make sure it doesn't burn.

Gently release the ice cream cake from the springform pan. Place extra apple pie filling on the top of the cake and drizzle caramel sauce over. Place the pie decorations and the pie wreath on top of the cake. Serve immediately.

Commonly Used Equipment

Cake Pans

Your best friend when it comes to baking these cakes will be your springform pan or push pan with 3-inch (8-cm) tall sides. Whichever pan you use, it's very important that the bottom is double wrapped in foil if you're baking in a water bath. And to keep it consistent, use hot water in the water bath every time—really hot water from your tap should work perfectly fine.

I use regular 2-inch (5-cm) pans when I'm baking single layers, but transfer them to a pastry ring or springform pan when I'm building up the layers.

Lining Material

I use parchment paper to prevent the baked layers from sticking to the pans. It also makes it very easy to transfer the cake from the baking pans to your serving tray.

For cakes where I add a layer of mousse or ice cream (any non-baked layer), I line the sides of the cake pan with 3- to 4-inch (8- to 10-cm) tall acetate paper, and then layer the filling. This way, I get nice and smooth sides when I remove the acetate paper. You can use parchment paper as well, but any moisture can wrinkle the parchment paper. Just remember to remove any lining material before serving the cake!

Mixers

Except for the buttercream, meringue layers and stabilized whipped cream, I always used my trusted hand mixer or balloon whisk for all the cakes in this book. A good hand mixer is a great investment. It's especially handy for the cheesecakes, where you don't want to overmix the cake batter.

Kitchen Scale

The importance of a simple kitchen scale cannot be overstated. All the dry ingredients that were used to bake these cakes were measured with a digital kitchen scale. The reason I use a scale and not cups is because the same ingredient—depending on the brand and other factors—can measure differently in the same cup. How you fill the measurement cup with a particular ingredient can also vary quite significantly from one person to the next, which can obviously have a big impact when it comes to baking. To avoid all that, measurements in terms of ounces and pounds (or grams and kilograms) will give you the most accurate and consistent results. And all you need for that is a basic digital scale that's very inexpensive and certainly much easier to use than cups.

Miscellaneous

Apart from the aforementioned main characters, a slew of role players also feature in any baker's kitchen: balloon whisk, spatulas, large metal spoons (to fold in egg whites), heatproof glass bowls (of varying sizes), metal bowls, regular spoons, sieves, measuring cups for liquid measurements and measuring spoons. And, of course, an oven.

Commonly Used Techniques

Cheesecake

Cheesecakes are really easy to make (and insanely delicious to eat!). There are just a couple of sound practices that you need to get a crack-free, silky smooth surface on your cheesecake, making all your friends and family jealous, every time.

The more air you incorporate into a cheesecake, the more it will expand in the oven as it bakes. But then as soon as it comes out of the oven, it will start deflating. A cheesecake is like an ego—too much expanding and too much deflating can cause it to crack. Here's how to get your cheesecake swag just right.

Do not overmix the cheesecake batter: Only mix just enough to combine the ingredients, especially the eggs (because eggs add a lot of air to the cheesecake batter). That first step of mixing cream cheese is really important. This ensures the cream cheese is nice and smooth and is receptive to other ingredients. The eggs are added right at the end and mixed on low speed (for larger cheesecakes) or manually with a balloon whisk (for smaller cheesecakes), until just combined.

Add some cornstarch: I add some cornstarch (cornflour) when I make cheesecake layers. This gives the cheesecake some structure and stability and helps avoid cracks.

Regulate the temperature: Sudden temperature changes make the cheesecake rise rapidly or collapse, which can cause cracks. This is why baking a cheesecake in a water bath is a good idea. The water bath regulates the heat better, and bakes the cake evenly. You can, of course, bake a cheesecake without a water bath, but this causes the sides to bake faster (resulting in crinkled sides), and also increases the chances of cracks on the surface.

What if there are still cracks on your cheesecake? Who cares! No one's judging. Just slather some ganache or whipped cream on top and serve that bad boy! As long as it tastes amazing, no one's going to complain. (If they still do, you should change friends. Just kidding . . . maybe.)

Meringue and Pavlova

Meringues and pavlovas are extremely interesting layers to include in your secret-layer cakes. Just egg whites and sugar make up the base for these layers. Meringues are crispy and light, add a sweet crunch and can be eaten as is (meringue cookies, kisses and so on), crushed into desserts (see the Basil Berry Eton Mess Cake [page 91]) or used as whole layers in cakes (see the Ceylon Cinnamon Chocolate Meringue Cake [page 97]). They are also the base for some beautiful French desserts where ground nuts are folded into the meringue to make nutty, crispy, sweet layers.

Pavlovas are an Australian and New Zealand classic (there's a longstanding "debate" on which of the two countries is the true birthplace of pavlova, which is unlikely to ever be settled). It's the vinegar that gives pavlova that irresistible marshmallowy center.

Cornstarch acts as a stabilizer for meringues and pavlovas, too. Pavlovas are taller than meringues, and the combination of vinegar and cornstarch in pavlovas helps keep them crisp on the outside and soft, light and marshmallowy on the inside, unlike meringues, which are crispy most of the way through. However, if you bake a pavlova too long, it will eventually turn into a chewy meringue.

Different bakers have somewhat different techniques that they follow and swear by to get meringues and pavlovas just right. The following tips and techniques have helped me get perfect meringues and pavlovas for my desserts.

Do not overbeat: Overbeating will cause meringues, and especially pavlovas, to collapse as they cool.

Make sure sugar is dissolved: Undissolved sugar in the meringue will cause the meringue or pavlova to "weep" or seep—meaning beads of moisture will form on the baked surface or there'll be sugar syrup puddling below the meringue.

Bake until crispy: Crispy meringues are very easy to make, but the length of time it takes for a meringue to crisp up varies from oven to oven. If your kitchen is extra humid, then the meringue will take longer to bake. The size and thickness can vary the baking time, too. One way to check whether your meringue is done is to gently lift it off the parchment paper. It is more likely to lift up cleanly when the meringue is dry. The extra cooling time in the oven will help the meringue dry out as well. Remember that moisture is a crispy meringue killer, so store the completely cooled meringues in airtight containers.

Meringue Topping

There are three ways to make meringue topping that you can use on your pies or to make buttercream: French meringue, Swiss meringue and Italian meringue.

French meringue: Here you whisk the egg whites and add the sugar while whisking, until the mixture is thick and glossy.

Swiss meringue: Here egg whites and sugar are whisked together over a pot of simmering water (a double boiler) until the sugar is dissolved in the egg whites. Then the egg whites are whisked in a mixer until the mixture cools down and is thick and glossy.

Italian meringue: Here you boil sugar and water to make a sugar syrup, which is then drizzled into the egg white mixture, while it's being whisked, until thick and glossy.

I have only used the Swiss meringue in this book when making meringues to top pies and cakes (such as the Lemon Meringue Bombe Alaska and the S'mores Brownie Pie). I just prefer that technique more, although the Italian meringue is also very stable. The French meringue, however, is not recommended for topping pies and cakes because it does result in some weeping.

Gelatin

I use gelatin as the setting agent for some of the layers in these cakes. You can find gelatin in powdered form or as leaf gelatin. Because the powder is the easiest to find, that's what I have used exclusively. One packet of gelatin is usually about 2¼ teaspoons (10 g).

Before you can use the gelatin, you need to first let it "bloom," whereby each gelatin granule is saturated and softened in water. This is true of powdered gelatin or leaf gelatin. To dissolve the gelatin, you need to heat it, either by adding it to a heated mixture or by heating the bloomed gelatin in the microwave or in a saucepan. It's very important that you don't let the gelatin boil, because this will interfere with its ability to set.

Brownies and Blondies

All the brownies and blondies in this book were made with a hand mixer or a balloon whisk. I used bittersweet chocolate for the brownies, which lends a richer, deeper chocolate flavor. I used dark brown sugar for all the blondies.

Stabilized Whipped Cream

Using stabilized whipped cream means that I can decorate a cake and keep it in the fridge until I am ready to serve. Freshly whipped cream tastes a lot better than readymade whipped cream, but it doesn't keep for long because the cream separates into a dry foam and a liquid. That's certainly not the topping you want on that gorgeous cake of yours. So adding a stabilizer like gelatin means that you can decorate your cake ahead of time with beautifully whipped cream swirls that last a lot longer than regular whipped cream.

Popping Candy (Pop Rocks)

These are some of my favorite candies to play around with. They are carbonated candies with carbon dioxide (CO_2) trapped inside the crystals. When they come into contact with heat or moisture, they release the pressurized carbon dioxide in a fizzy, popping reaction. It's the ultimate surprise in desserts!

Popping candy can be found in the brand Pop Rocks, which comes in different flavors. However, I prefer to use unflavored and uncoated popping candy. If you're using uncoated popping candy, please note that it can get soggy faster and lose its fizz and pop. Keep it frozen for a few hours and only thaw when you're ready to serve.

If you'd like to have popping candy last longer, try to find chocolate- or cocoa butter–coated popping candy This coating protects the candy from being exposed to moisture. If you'd like to coat your own popping candy (as I did), simply use melted cocoa butter. Once coated, the candy can be stored in the freezer to set and then broken (carefully) into smaller pieces. You don't need to coat popping candy when you make popping candy chocolate bark.

Acknowledgments

A huge thank you to my husband, Kasun, first and foremost. To say that none of this would be possible without your fierce and unrelenting support is a colossal understatement. Thank you for believing in me when no one else did, thank you for inspiring me and encouraging me to pursue my dreams, thank you for giving me the confidence I needed, every time I needed it. Thank you for being my taste tester, my sounding board, my occasional and disgruntled dishwasher and my best friend!

Thank you to my mother, for teaching me how to bake my first cake—a lesson that I never forgot. Thank you to my mother and father for being my taste testers and enduring my early experiments in the kitchen. Thank you to my sister, Ganu, for being my first dishwasher, taste tester and cheerleader.

Thank you to all my food blogger friends in my support group. Your company, your understanding, your appreciation and your constant words of encouragement mean so much more to me than you will ever know. It helps that you are all such positively wonderful people with giant hearts!

And last but not least, thank you to my publisher, Page Street. Thank you to Marissa and Meg, in particular, for being so accommodating and supportive, for putting up with all my questions and for all the help in writing this book. It goes without saying that none of this would be possible without them.

About the Author

Dini Kodippili is the writer, food photographer, recipe developer and creative force behind the blog theflavorbender.com. Born in Sri Lanka, she grew up in New Zealand and lived and worked in Australia before her current pit stop in the United States, where she now lives with her husband and currently-nonexistent-but-soon-to-be-acquired dog. She loves to share recipes on her blog that bring together different flavors, textures and food cultures in new and creative ways. She's particularly passionate about breakfast and brunch food and dessert of any kind, and will talk about it all day with anyone willing to listen. A self-professed nerd and food geek, Dini hopes to make you as intensely excited about cooking and baking as she is. Or at least try. Visit her at theflavorbender.com.

Index